Long Distance Triathlon Memoir 2

Jason Pegler

chipmunkapublishing
the mental health publisher

Jason Pegler

Published by
Chipmunkapublishing
United Kingdom

http://www.chipmunkapublishing.com

Copyright © 2015 Jason Pegler

ISBN   978-1-78382-184-6

Chipmunkapublishing gratefully acknowledge the support of Arts Council England.

Have you ever achieved something that you once thought was impossible? Go on have a think for a moment... Yes you have... Of course, you have... Everyone has... I hope... Think back to how you achieved it? You had to actually take the first steps and actually do it. I bet you didn't just daydream about it or you would never have achieved it. I first saw the ultimate one-day endurance event – the Ironman on television in 1984 when I was 9 years old. I thought that one day I would do it and completely forgot about the event until July 2012 when by chance I bumped into an Ironman veteran and saw a once in a lifetime opportunity staring me in the face.

In my memoir Long Distance Triathlon Memoir – How I Became a Man of Iron with 11 Months training, I described how I went from a complete novice to Ironman and completed my first Ironman in Klagenfurt in July 2013.
That book ends with me finishing Klagenfurt safely and deciding I wanted to enter another Ironman event the following year, Ironman Frankfurt. I vowed to be a better athlete the following year and mentioned that I was finally going to take 2 weeks off training by going to Lanzarote on holiday with my family.

Downtime – The importance of switching off:

Going to Lanzarote was fantastic. Twelve days on holiday with no training and some great family time with my partner and children. What a physical and mental release. Training for Ironman all year round is extremely tough and then the actual race itself is so physically and mentally draining that switching off is very important. When thinking about other things you can recharge your batteries and then go into the new season invigorated and mentally fresh.

Competing in my first Ironman was more exhausting than I thought. It's such a long day no matter how hard you train. It's really the ultimate test of survival and perseverance.

The aftermath of finishing my first Ironman was far more draining than I thought as well. There was the exhilaration of finishing, the disappointment in not achieving the time I set out to, the physical and mental recovery and the analyzing of what I did well and what I could have done better, the questioning whether all the sacrifices were worth it and the wondering whether I would be prepared to go through all the training and pain again for one more finish line moment and what comes with it.

This book tells the story of my training and race day for my second Ironman that took place in July 2014. In June 2013 I had finished my first ever Ironman in 13 hours and 17 minutes after 11 months swimming, cycling and running. Crossing the line I felt like I was superhuman. There were times during the race that I felt like a broken man but I managed to rally for the last 10km and cross the finish line strong. I had hoped for a time of 12 hours. The day after the race I was not sure if I really wanted to do another Ironman but 24 hours after that all I wanted to do was go faster next time around and finish in the time that I thought I was capable of.

I daydreamed about racing in Kona and being the oldest Ironman World champion ever. That really was absolute madness but it almost took me to believe the impossible to even have the confidence to focus and train for the Ironman in the first place. The yearning to be world champion is only ever likely to happen if I am reincarnated into another body. Apparently it takes 10 years to peak in Ironman and I would have to accept that my talent is limited. Of course some people have more talent than others, some are prepared to push themselves more than others and some are more dedicated than others.

I was 38 when I did my first Ironman the same age as when Craig Alexander won his 3rd Hawaii title in 2011. We have something in common, hopefully more... I'd only really know what I was capable of physically if I went for a quicker time and then came up with a training plan for it. For that I needed to sit down with my great coach Nick Kinsey (see mallorcaman.co.uk).

On my own whim I decided to get in touch with some of the greats of Ironman past and present and pick their brains so I could learn more about how I could be the best athlete I could be whilst maintaining an equilibrium with my partner, be the best dad I could be, continue being an effective social entrepreneur, a good partner, a good citizen and enjoy life to its fullest....

This journey was to take me to places that I could never imagine... Pain... Laughter... Euphoria. It's a roller coaster journey and I hope it mirrors your love for long distance triathlon as much as mine or encourages you to do your first swim, bike and run.

So, to recap my first Ironman race in Austria I had completed in 13 hrs and 18 minutes. My time splits were 1hr 34minutes on the swim, 6hr 13 minutes on the bike and then 5hrs 8 minutes on the marathon. Now I wanted to do another one and go quicker but first I needed to recover.

Nick sent me a text to guide me on my recovery, post Ironman Austria i.e. Klagenfurt.

From Monday reverse taper. I.e. do last week's sessions before the race.

Week after do the second week before race. Etc....

So 3rd week do the training set for the 1st week of taper. Generally you can cut run and increase swim. I will set a fuller/calculated schedule when I get back.

For recovery drink lots of red bush tea or green tea.

Eat a higher protein diet than normal. Have a bedtime protein drink, like SIS Nocte, maxi muscle protein or chocolate soya milk.

Only do this high protein steak, fish, and nuts diet for two weeks or you will get fat! Then resume normal daily diet routine.

Cheers Nicky Boy

So I did what Nick said post Ironman with Strawberry Maxi muscle protein shakes to go to sleep with for 2 weeks. I took 3 days off training and then felt like going on the turbo and swimming. I did not feel like running at all. The marathon had taken its toll on me in Klagenfurt. Now I knew what Nick meant when he said it was the death march and to treat it as 4 x 10km's and then give everything the last 2km. I figured if I improved my swimming then I would save time and energy in my next Ironman and also figured if I improved my bike endurance then I would run better next time around. Also I knew that my body was developing as an athlete and that in the three sports my muscles were developing and my skills and strength were gradually improving the more training that I did.

It was great to spend less time training and more time with the family. It was also great when everyone I asked saw me and asked me how the race went. This included many of the parents at the school where my son went. It was nice to tell them how I had achieved my goal of finishing safely. They would also all ask me if I was going to do another one. I said I was going to which made me accountable and more likely to follow through. I just had not decided which one to do yet. Nick had suggested Frankfurt or Challenge Roth as great races to do. Fast courses with great atmosphere's. I was also looking at other Ironman events including Nice, Sweden, Lanzarote, Zurich or Denmark. The timing of the Denmark race did not really fit in with my family commitments. Nick said that Nice and Lanzarote did not fit my body shape as they were both really hilly and I am 6ft 3 ½ inches tall. Switzerland was also quite hilly and Sweden didn't really fit in with timing either for my family and potential vacations.

Within a few weeks I had made my mind up. I decided to book Frankfurt. Nick said that it was a great move as it was the best-supported Ironman race in Europe. He had done it a few times. Once he came 18th overall so I was in the right hands. We set a goal for an 11-hour finish, which was quite ambitious, but I was pretty determined to give it my best shot.

The predicted splits were something like.
Swim 1 hr. 20 m
Bike 5 hrs 40 m
Run 3hrs 53 minutes
Transition totals 7 minutes

In fact I thought I could go even quicker. Nick was keeping my feet on the ground and giving me realistic goals. We decided to make my warm up race Wimblewall. That is a really tough 70.3 and was 3 weeks before Frankfurt.

I was pretty conscious of my weight throughout training and racing. On the 6th august 2013 my weight was 88.4. Kilos. It went down to 85.6 kilos by the 8th of august after 2 days training. I was 85 kilos for Ironman Klagenfurt

Back In Training

7th august 2013 back in training. Swim 45 and 30m run.

I decided to enter another race in September 2013 to keep me ticking over. It turned out to be my first sprint triathlon so I knew I had the endurance for it.

As the weeks after Klagenfurt went by the euphoria of finishing declined and training boredom set in. It was great to set another goal of another Ironman, even better to have some time off with no training and great to go to Spain and forget about Swimming and Cycling for a while and just get back into running to build up my confidence again.

First I was off to Spain for 10 days with the family to stay with the Spanish Grandparents. My partner Sonia is Spanish and her mum and dad live in Spain so we go and see them once or twice a year and stay with them. I had no bike or swim kit with me there so ran most days and did some gym work.

I did not do exactly as Nick said but just felt like being a bit different. I really wanted to see how fast I could over 5km and 10km. This is not how you are meant to train for an Ironman i.e. a fast 5 or 10km but this is what I felt like doing at the time. I also had to be mindful of the traffic as I was running across roads in Burgos in the

North of Spain, which is quite a busy city although very picturesque and hot in the summer. Each time I took the same running route:

Aug 25 - 10km 51min 10seconds
Aug 27 - 10km 49min 20 seconds
Aug 29 - 46 min 40 seconds. First 5km in 22m 30sec.
Aug 31 - first 5km in 20min 53 sec.
Second 5km in 27minutes.
Sept 2 - 7.2 miles in 60 minutes. 1st 3.6miles and 2nd 3.6 miles both in 30minutes.

On my phone I tapped in some worst case and best-case scenarios for different lengthened triathlons. It showed my belief/ability at the time:

Goals 2013/14
Sprint
Swim 750m 15m-19m
20k bike 30m-35m
5k run 23m- 22m
Transition 4m-m
1hr 12m- 1hr 23m

Olympic
Swim 40-35m
Bike 1hr 15-1hr 8m
Run 54 min-50m
Transition 4m-3m
2hrs 53m-2hr 36m.....

Half
Swim 45m
Bike 2hrs 30
Run 1hr 50m
Trans 5
5hrs 10m

My First Sprint Triathlon

By the middle of September 2013 I was back in my next race. I was quite excited about entering my first ever Sprint Triathlon. I had tried to enter the Olympic distance but it had already sold out so settled for the Sprint distance. I had plenty of confidence going into it, as I knew that by being an Ironman I could easily cover the distance. The question was, how much speed did I have?

The weather on the day itself was quite sunny. I drove down on my own. The competitors were in waves of 100 athletes and my wave did not start until the early afternoon. This was to be my first race ever after 8.15 am.

There were thousands of people watching the event and hundreds of competitors all over the place. I got all my gear together, looked at the transition entries and exits and then made my way down to the start with my wetsuit on. This was going to be the first time that I had ever swam in the Thames.

There were 100 of us lining up all in number order for our wave. It was quite a cool feeling warming up. I knew my swim was going to be slow but it didn't look very long compared to an Ironman swim, my plan was to go full out on the bike and overtake everyone and then go as hard as I could on the run but keep a little bit back for the last half a mile or so.

The gun or horn went off and we were away. I was swimming ok but was gradually being overtaken by most people and then when I looked up I was definitely swimming too far sideways. The week before I had emailed Harry Wiltshire the Ironman professional and brilliant swimmer and arranged a swim lesson but I had not managed to get his advice before this race. This was a pity, as I really needed his skills.

I came out of the 750-metre swim in 16 minutes 57 seconds. Wearing my Garmin 910 I moved to transition mode and over took half a dozen people on the way up to transition. It was a few hundred metres. Then I got on my bike and started to really put on the gas. I went on just about the biggest gear I could apart from the first couple of minutes as I got used to being on the bike. The course was pretty flat but there were a lot of people in the way and there were some sharp turns. There were several laps to cover – the bike course was 42.2km all together. I came close to falling off having to balance like a one footed giraffe a couple of times on the first lap but once I got used to the course I managed to time the sharp corners better.

Fortunately people were riding on the correct side most of the time, so it was quite easy to power past a lot of people at a time and then drop in when appropriate. Along the course I must have overtaken hundreds of people and only a handful went past me and they were going at a really fast pace. Most of them that would have been over taking me would have been under 1hr for 40km at a guess.

I was pleased with my bike time, which was in the top 10-15% of the competitors'.

I felt strong going into transition and was interested to see how good I could go on the run. The run was 2 laps. There was a great atmosphere, which I could take in more on the bike. On the bike I could see great London land marks but was focusing on where I was going that it was all a bit of a blur. On the run you could hear people cheering people on. I took a sip of water at one or two of the aid stations. By the second lap I was just grabbing a bit of water, having a sip and then pouring it on my head as I was pretty hot by then.

I gave it my all on the sprint finish and my run split turned out to be 21 minutes. I was pretty pleased considering it was after a swim and a bike. I was even more pleased when I got home and discovered that the mega strong coffees that I had thought I had that morning before going out were actually decaffeinated coffee.

I was just like any other Triathlete. Clinging on for any reason or possibility that could enable me to go quicker next time. I ate some food after the event and then got home and had my usual over eating frenzy the day after a race. My 5 year old boy, Oscar and 3 year old girl, Anna were quite impressed by the medal which was nice. I got some good feedback from Nick.

My overall time and position was in the top 15% of entrants so I was pleased with that.

I then set about training for my next race, which was a month later in October 2013.

It would be my second Standard Duathlon at Chilham. Twelve months before it had been my very first event. This time I knew I would do better but how much better would be the big question.

Harry Wiltshire Ironman Pro and my new Swim Coach

Before that I decided to go and meet Harry Wiltshire in Leeds and have my first Swim lesson with a pro. It turned out to exceed my expectations. In my first Ironman memoir I describe how Nick had turned me from being an embarrassment to somebody who could swim, Dan Bullock (A swim coach who Nick had recommended) had given me a bit of confidence to go quicker and from Harry I was looking for some magic which was exactly what I got.

He met me at the train station and we walked up to the Leeds University swimming pool. Harry is such a nice guy. He is really chatty and down to earth. He is also very passionate about Triathlon. What struck me was how lean he looked. That morning he had been swimming with the elite training Triathletes that included Alistair and Johnny Brownlee. Olympic Gold and Bronze Medalists and both World ITU Champions. Watching me swim was going to be a bit of a come down but I was paying him so every little helps I guess.

He videoed my stroke. After the session we went through the stroke and how it looked at the start of the lesson, at different stages and at the end. Harry pointed out what was wrong with it at the start and where it had improved by the end. Seeing myself swimming was embarrassing and fascinating. Embarrassing as in my head I swam a lot neater and more elegantly than I actually did and fascinating as I could see how I was improving by listening to what he said and then doing what he said during the lesson.

At the start of the lesson he got me to swim 25 x 8 metres to look at my stroke. Then he would tell me how I swam, what was ok and then what I could do better. Then he would get me to focus on one thing for a couple of lengths, stop me and then reiterate the point or explain it again in more details. The lesson went on like this for an hour and I definitely started to feel more confident afterwards. Then we had around 45 minutes one to one looking at the videos etc. and that was it.

The 3 things I was to focus on after my very first lesson

were to swim wider with both arms as my hands were going to far inwards, start the catch earlier and in a different hand position and focus on pulling the water backwards and inwards instead of just back and down. After the lesson I spoke to harry for a bit about my ideas of setting up a new Triathlon company to help the pros make more money and he was pretty interested and complimentary about it. Then I gave him a bit of advice about how much I thought he should charge for his swimming lessons and coaching and we agreed to meet up for another swimming lesson sometime in the future and I would keep him informed of my progress.

Just a week after my swim lesson with Harry I was able to notice the massive improvement in my times. On the Sept 26th of September my 3km swim time was 81 minutes. Then after that I had my lesson with Harry and my next 3km swim time was 68 minutes. Within a couple of months I had managed to get it down to 63 minutes. This did miracles for my self-belief and what was also significant was that I was less tired coming out of the pool as I was wasting less energy and feeling more confident.

As I got in touch with Harry and had such a positive experience that I decided to chase up some of the Triathlon and Ironman super heroes. I had a SKYPE call with Tim Don, which was quite interesting. He was advertising looking to coach people in Triathlon220. I was happy being coached by Nick but just wanted to have a chat with Tim and see how he approached coaching and racing. We discussed the possibility that instead of coaching me for my sessions that we would have an occasional call and that I would pay him for that. However I contacted him several times after that via SKYPE and email and he never replied. Weird.

Rachel Joyce Consultancy

Not one to be held back I decided to go for it and contacted Rachel Joyce. We had an introductory call and it was really interesting. She was being coached by the legend 6 times Ironman world champion Dave Scott (as was Tim Don as well actually). Rachel had come 6th, 5th and 4th in Kona 3 years in a row, followed by a disappointing race the year after but then won Ironman Texas and was one of the favourites for The Ironman World championships in 2013.

I had an initial call with Rachel around about August and then let her focus on the World Championships. She did great coming 2nd overall. Only the amazing Mirinda Carfrae beat her by running the fastest ever marathon split from a female Ironman Pro. Rachel and I agreed to having one consultancy call a month that I could record, with one or two emails in between to prepare the call.

Notes from my first One to One coaching session with Rachel Joyce – October 2013

10 hour split
1hr 10 swim
5hr 20 bike
3hr 30 min run (this is too quick for ironman run)
Transition 10 minutes

Massage...
Keep up strength work gym/core – 3 x 20 minutes a week. Core work/planks.. Dave Scott big advocate of that. Of course, Rachel is trained by Dave Scott whilst she tells me this... Just something I did not do from December to March at least... Rachel said that most

people suffer on the run as their core is not strong enough.

It was around this time that I was still over thinking everything. I was only 16 months into the sport and wanting to learn everything about it. Rachel said that she had been overwhelmed with information at one time and that it took her a while to realise it. Nick had told me the same thing yet this addiction I had to the sport made me want to learn more and more every day. It wasn't really until after Frankfurt had finished in July 2014 that I was able to take a more relaxed approach to all of it.

Anyway a bit of an aside there. What next ? I hear you ask ?

My Second Chilham Duathlon October 2013

Chilham castle strategy set by Nick:

Run go 175-180 first half
Then up to 190 2nd half
Bike - hold off 10% uphills - some drink on flatter bits.
Take gel half way through bike
Burn 2nd half of bike flat
2nd run - go full out 180-190

Going into my second Chilham duathlon I was a much better athlete and a lot more experienced than first time around. I had a look at the entrants on the day of the race. Lucy Gossage that name looked familiar. That's one person I won't be beating I thought.

It was 8.15 am and freezing as usual. This time I was equipped with some proper cross-country Saucony trainers. At Chilham in October 2012 I came 46th out of

112 overall. That was my first competitive race so not bad. I was prepared for the mega muddy course this time around, stronger, fitter and quicker.

The first few hundred metres surprised me. I was in the lead. What on earth was I doing. I was the first one off the grass and looked at my Garmin less than 6 minute pace I better slow down or I will run out of batteries somewhere later on in the race.

I got into my rhythm and felt good. Two laps of 5 km and I was surprised how near to the front I was. Only 10-20 people in front of me and some of them were doing a relay. I finished the first 10km run in 49 minutes that was over 4 minutes quicker than the previous year.

Then it was time to get on the bike. I lost a few seconds with my shades as they were so dark I could not see anything in the rain so I put them in my pocket and never used them after that. It was one of the only pieces of kit I had bought myself without Nick's advice so just shows how important a coach can be when you start out in Triathlon.

I got into a wrong gear going up hill at the start but still managed to overtake a woman I recognized form the year before. I had been behind hear the year before when her shoe fell off about half a mile and I ran by but then a few minutes later she had overtaken me again and I do not think I saw her again during the race. This time I was already ahead of her on the bike.

Then on the same hill as I went to the right slightly having to stand being in the wrong gear some guy over took me and we nearly collided. That was close. He was going for it. He was the only person who overtook me the whole 40km on the bike. I managed to overtake a few people but not that many as I was quite near the front. Later on I found out that he was doing the bike leg only as part of a relay team.

Going back into T2 I had a quick transition and managed to run the whole 5km this time. I had finished 5th in my age group and 15th overall which included 6 relay teams so 9th overall. I was 20 minutes quicker than the year before. Now I was starting to feel like a real athlete.

This gave me great confidence going into my winter training. My next race was going to be my second time at the ballbuster but first I was going to have a tough test. The hardest sportive in the UK the Hell of the Ashdown 110km of hills, hills and more hills.

During the Winter I did not want to go out on the bike at all. I'd swim twice a week, go on the turbo 2 or 3 times a week and do 2-3 runs a week – one of them a long run.

Nutrition - Laura Church and Phil The Power Taylor

Having not got the time I wanted in Ironman Austria I was looking into anything I could about improving my nutrition. Nick always said to have a balanced diet and you'll be fine. Sometimes I just thought that I lacked the natural ability that someone like Nick had as an athlete and with two young children to look after and starting late as an athlete I felt that anything extra I could learn about nutrition could only be a good thing. That's when I came across nutritionist Laura Church. She also happened to be the nutritionist of one of my heroes the greatest darts player of all time - Phil Taylor. She had been Phil's nutritionist for a couple of years helping him lose weight and eat healthier whilst he continued to maintain his number one status.

Well what does darts have to do with Ironman? Nothing really except that is that Phil Taylor is no ordinary darts player. In fact he is no ordinary sportsman. He is no ordinary champion. World champion and no ordinary multiple world champion if there is such a thing. Phil the Power Taylor is 16 times world champion. Yes, that is 16 times. There is no other sportsman at any sport in the modern era that is anywhere near to winning 16 world championships.

Phil Taylor is probably the greatest sportsman of all, alive in the world today. My thoughts were that therefore there is nobody who knows more about winning and more about achieving one's full potential than Phil Taylor.

I contacted Laura. I told her I wanted to achieve my potential at Ironman and be the best athlete I can be. She was inspirational. She was a very talented athlete herself. She represented Great Britain at Judo at all age groups and was trained by Superstar champion Brian Jacks. At one time she could even do more squat thrusts in one minute than Brian Jacks himself. 120 I think she said. She also won multiple bodybuilding championships including coming second overall in the World Championships. I told her of my goals and also of my big ambition to meet probably my greatest sporting hero Phil Taylor. She said to sort the nutrition plan out first and then she would speak to Phil and see if he could meet me. I said I didn't want anything from him. I just wanted to meet him and ask him how to become so successful at something and remain so dedicated. I knew that to reach the peak of my Ironman potential it would take me a lot more than 2 years probably 6-10 years if my body, mind and will power were strong enough.

I paid Laura for some Consultancy, which included a daily nutrition plan, ongoing support and One to One training session. I arrived at her house where she has her own gym. We spoke for a few minutes and then it was time for the gym session. As I walked in I saw dozens of her bodybuilding and judo trophies on display and the World Team Darts Championships won the previous year by Phil Taylor and Adrian Lewis.

The training session was built all around core strength. It was hard work, especially using the TRX training. I tried it once and ended up exhausted.

I'd never really know why I did not get the time I wanted in Ironman Austria. I was aiming for less than 12 hours and achieved 13hrs 18 minutes. Where had I lost those 80 minutes? Well I had the penalty on the bike, which mentally floored me, it was absolutely boiling and I was not used to racing in that heat for such a long time. I was experimenting with my nutrition and that can often take a while to get right in races and mentally I had just now done a race that long so it was harder than I ever envisaged.

Was my core simply not strong enough? Is that why I went so slowly in the marathon in Austria ? Was my slow marathon in the Ironman down to having a weak core, as Rachel Joyce believed was the case with many slow run splits in Ironman racing. Or was I just mentally weaker than I envisaged on race day than prior to race day?

After an hours training with Laura I was exhausted. I knew my core could be a lot stronger. Lets just put it that way. Then after I freshened up we sat down and went through my eating plan. I had prepared a food diary prior to my visit. Here it is:

Food diary November 2013 for Laura Church nutritionist

Thursday:

Pint of water 6.45
Protein shake with milk 7.00
Coffee 7.05
Glass of water 9.45
3 poached eggs on brown granary toast with can of baked beans - 10.00am
Coffee 10.50
60 minutes turbo 11-12
Glass of milk and banana 12.05
Glass of water 12.15
Cheese sandwich with butter and brown bread 12.25 - felt bloated for 45 minutes afterwards

Handful of raisins 1.30.
Glass of water 3.00
Glass of water 3.45
Cup of Camomille tea 3.50
Clementine 4.45
Feel healthier now...
Glass of water 5.27pm
5.50-6.05 big Salad with avocado, couscous, raisins, spring onion, croutons, Parmesan, olive oil, Caesar salad sauce.
Half a glass of water 6.08
Felt a bit bloated for 10 minutes now feel good.
6.20 Camomille tea
7pm yoghurt
9pm bit more salad
9.30 glass of water

Friday
6.25am glass of water
6.30 am organic porridge

6.40 am 1 maxi muscle powdered protein milkshake
9.30-10.02 1500km swim
10.18 banana. 10.20-10.25 Protein shake with milk. 20 minutes later. Feel good...
10.45 half pint of water
12.00 cup of coffee
12.18 glass of water
12.40 glass of water
1.20 glass of water
I piece of garlic bread
2.00 tuna Nicoise salad
Half a litre of water
2.55 decaf coffee
4.35 2 slices of ham
Sips of water whilst driving quarter glass
6.20 grapes 25 pip less
6.25 banana
6.40 small garden salad - lettuce, tomatoes, sweet corn, olives, cucumber, tomatoes.
6.45-7.00 lentils, morzilla, onion, garlic, red peppers, courgette, canned tomatoes, chorizo, chicken stock, Parmesan cheese,

Sat - rest day no training
5.30 two pieces of whole meal toast and honey. Feel fine
7.30 coffee
8.15 glass of water
8.25am two pieces of wholemeal toast and honey. Feel fine.
9.00am glass of water
9.45am half a banana
10 2 glasses of water
10.15 coffee
10.30-45 2 glasses of water
Stomach ache - since 2nd coffee.
11.35 1 clementine
11.50 lentils left over from yesterday

1.05 vanilla yoghurt activia
1.15 18 mini raw tomatoes 3 of 5 veg of the day
1.40 2 rich tea biscuits
2.25 20 raisins. 10 almonds.
4.00 3 Weetabix and skimmed milk
Feel fine
4.15 handful of almonds a dozen
4.40 raisins 20
6.30 lamb balti and coconut rice. Sip of water.
9.00 protein shake
9.30 protein shake
Sleep

Sunday
5.50 protein shake
7.30 coffee
8.00am 90 minute easy run 9.5 miles.
9.35 protein shake and 20 raisins
9.40 3 pieces of honey on whole meal seeded toast.
Feel fine
9.50 1 glass of water
10.25 2 pints of water
11.00 1/2 pint of water.
11.30 coffee
11.40 glass of water
12.20 pint of water, granola bar and boiled egg sandwich
1.50 2 danone pro biotic yoghurt drinks. Tiny.
3.00-500 1 pint of water. 10 chips (at a kids party).
5.00 10 raisins. 3 Chicken drum sticks, 1/2 plate of broccoli, roasted tomatoes and peppers, potato gratin with béchamel sauce.
Feel fine after
5.20 pro biotic yoghurt and vanilla yoghurt.
6.30 10 almonds. 10 raisins. Pro biotic yoghurt. 1 banana. 50 raw carrot sticks. 2 1/2 Weetabix with skimmed milk

After sitting down with Laura's for a few hours I was quickly becoming much more aware of what I was eating and why I was possibly feeling so tired. Laura backed everything up with scientific evidence as well so it was very reassuring. I agreed to eat more often, every 2-3 hours in the main, have more protein in my diet, eat more nuts to stop my over eating. Have mixed nuts in the car in case I felt like binge eating. I agreed to eat smaller lunch and smaller evening meals and combine protein, carbs and water-based foods with every meal. I also embarked upon a specific daily vitamin intake that Laura suggested which consisted of taking Vitamin C, Vitamin B Complex, Vitamin D, Glucosamine And Chondroitin, L-Glutamine and Omega 3,6 and 9.

I also stopped drinking dairy products all together and moved over to almond milk. After a few days I actually stopped farting for good. Unbelievable how on the days I had a bit of cheese that the farts would come back. As Laura said most people become lactose intolerant when they get older.

Laura and I kept in touch by text and she looked forward to being one of my key team members in helping me become the best athlete I could become. I was starting to like having a bigger team around me. Nick was my coach and main man. He set my daily training sessions and I would text him daily on how I was doing. I had just discovered Harry Wiltshire as my swim coach. I had Laura Church as my nutritionist. I had just agreed with Rachel Joyce to have a monthly consultancy call about my Frankfurt goal for July 2014.

Laura said that once I took the vitamins daily and adjusted what I ate that I would recover quicker, train better and have more energy on a daily basis. I wanted to believe this and sure enough within a few weeks I started to feel a lot less tired and had more energy. I needed something to motivate me and to drive me forward as Ironman Frankfurt was a long time away. It was not until July 2014.

A Day With Darts Legend Phil Taylor

One day I had a call from Laura Church that left me in awe. "I've spoken to Phil about your goals and he said he doesn't want any money and he is happy to meet you and have a chat with you". How cool was that? I was going to meet my Sporting Hero! Phil, The Power Taylor. I met up with Laura in London and we took the train and then a taxi to where Phil was staying.

He had rented a house out for a couple of weeks nearby London as the World Darts Championships was on. He was already through to the second round and had a few days off. We rang the door and it was a bit surreal. Phil Taylor answered the door. "Hi Laura, hi ya fella, come on in... take a seat... make yourself at home... I sat in the lounge and Phil and Laura walked through to the kitchen and caught up for a couple of minutes. Then they came back in and Phil said. Hi Jason, pleased to meet you. Laura tells me you're an Ironman athlete... Fair play to yeah... That sounds tough... What would you like to talk about ? I am here to help.

I was blown away. Its 2.00pm in the afternoon and I am sat down talking to Phil Taylor. The conversation switches between us talking about darts and Phil's preparation, to Laura's nutrition business and then Ironman training. Every now and then I ask Phil the same kind of question but in a slightly different way. "Why are you so good at darts compared to everyone else?".

Jason I will give you one word "Dedication". That's the difference. That's the difference between the rest and me... Well that was it in the early days... Now its getting my mind right... doing the right thing... at the right times.... Being focused.... Belief... When it's flowing you do not need to think about it... you just play and the 180's go in and the double's go in.

Every five minutes or so the conversation is interrupted for a moment as someone walks past the lounge waving at Phil, shouting "the power" and he waves back. The guy is so famous. He has only rented the house out for a couple of weeks and lives hundreds of miles away and people recognize him when he is sat in the lounge! After about half an hour Laura closes the curtains so he can have a bit more privacy.

Its interesting hearing him talk about other darts players. He is totally relaxed one moment and then ultra competitive the next. It's almost like two different people talking. That must be the ingredient of a champion I am thinking to myself.

Mark Allen the 6 times World Ironman Champion talks about being in flow when racing. Jan Frodeno 2008 Olympic Triathlon Champion once said: "I look at everyone before the race and think you are going to have to have your best day ever to beat me".

As the afternoon goes on Phil shows me some of his favourite videos on you tube. He is cracking jokes every 5 minutes. The funniest video he shows is Mohammed Ali and Spike Milligan on some talk show. Wogan or something like that. Spike Milligan is telling some horror story for a few minutes and then comes to the end with the punch line and Mohammed Ali nearly jumps out of his seat. It's absolutely hilarious.

Listening to Phil was fascinating. One minute he is talking about someone in his family or friend and then the next sentence he is responding to a text coming through. This one is from Carl Froch, World Boxing Champion coming in or he is talking about a conversation he had with Ricky Hatton, Robbie Williams or Robbie Williams' Dad.

The afternoon turns into evening and gets even better when he then invites us out to dinner. We walk down the high street. As we cross a really busy road a car stops in the middle of it and three or four people start singing the darts theme tune and then they all start singing there's only one Phil Taylor. Then the wind suddenly picks up and the biggest dustbin I have ever seen blows across the road and is just about to go straight into Phil and I pick it up and put it back on the pavement. How bizarre.

We get to the restaurant and are the first people in it. I'm obsessing over what's on the menu as I am sat with my nutritionist and Laura says go on Jason you can have a night off you deserve it so I decide to have a couple of beers, as well. I am thinking it might loosen me up a bit and stop me being so serious. A couple of beers later and I had really lightened up and started to understand all of Phil's jokes. I spoke a bit about my publishing business and personal development experience and had a great time.

On the way back we got absolutely soaked and it was a good 10-minute walk in the downpour with a gale blowing outside. Phil didn't even have a coat on. I was thinking of giving him my coat as he had a game a few days later but I had training the next day as well.

Laura got a taxi home and I hung around for a bit. I got

a great photo of Phil and me together on my phone and then got a taxi back home. What a great day. Now I knew a bit more about the mind of a champion I had to put the winter training in and become one.

Phoning Dave Scott Ironman Legend

Meeting Phil made me realise more than ever that certain people are successful because they get on with it and do not procrastinate about anything.

With that thought in mind I thought I might as well get in touch with Dave Scott 6, times Ironman World Champion and the first guru of Ironman competition. I contacted him through his website and to my surprise his PA emailed back and arranged a phone call for the following week. Wow... Awesome.

The the call was more about Dave's coaching program as he is now a triathlon coach and my plan was definitely to stay with Nick until after Ironman Frankfurt. I just wanted to have a conversation with one of the greats, to lock in some more experience for the tough training and tough Ironman race ahead. When I spoke to Dave on the phone I did say I wanted to interview him in the future and he said that was cool.

I interviewed him a bit during him talking about his coaching. The start of the call was hilarious. I said "It's like speaking to god on the phone". Dave laughed and said "Jason, I'm just Dave". He spoke with great conviction about his beliefs in core training, swim, bike and run techniques, training and nutrition.

Much of the nutritional information was similar to Laura's although there were some key differences. Dave believed that once a day you needed to not eat for 3 hours. He also preferred coconut milk above all other types of milk. Both of them said not to eat too much bread. They both advocated mixing carbs and protein and lots of salad. They both said not to eat too much bread. Dave said no more than 2 slices a day and Laura said no more than 3 slices a day. Speaking to Dave Scott was incredibly motivating for my training. I knew that by speaking to him it would make me want to train even more. Dave is such a down to earth and nice guy. I planned to go out to Boulder, (in Colorado in America) sometime and meet him and join in his gym class with the likes of Rachel Joyce and Tim Don and some other great athletes. He also held swim and run sessions throughout the week so that would be an awesome holiday I could bring the kids and my Sonia to. We spoke about it but did not get round to doing it as training for a second Ironman was taking enough of my time and energy up anyway.

It is definitely hard to get a work, life, and fitness balance. The more you push the Ironman the more you have to be aware that you may become unbalanced in another area of your life. Fortunately I'd stopped watching television almost completely which helped. I was spending less time with my children than before my fitness frenzy but I was very lucky that I saw them more than most dads. I was definitely in a better mood in generally now I was super fit and eating better helped a lot as I became less fatigued and did have a better recovery in general.

I was very happy with my nutritionist Laura. I did speak to Laura about some of Dave's eating tips and she agreed with most of it. She said coconut milk was just as good as almond milk and to me it tasted better as well.

One powerful line, I remember from Dave is "Faith within self breeds the highest probability of success:"

He also said that one time he did not train for 21 days. This made me feel less guilty for missing a session because of illness or fatigue or just not fitting it in. However in my training for Frankfurt I was going to make sure that I gave it everything and worked even harder than my training for Klagenfurt.

Below are some notes from my conversations with Dave Scott. I hope you find them useful.

Dave Scott notes:

- Do not use the word pain - use the term barometer of discomfort and you have the ability to control this - speed down slow up, feel all different parts of your body one at a time, break it down into smaller psychological chunks, the race flows by very quickly as i thought like this while doing it. In the now......

- Use mantras to stay in control

- Dave uses visual

- List of should and have to do:
- Look at what i want to do

- I want to commit to being ironman world champion by October 2022.

- What would I like to do and be responsible for...

- Step by step, what can I control, be in the moment, as long as my goals were internally developed can get rid of the fear....

- Recognise your small accomplishments.....

- Don't lose that faith within...

- Goals every 2 weeks breakthrough workouts important...

- Up to 4-6 weeks if flowing along

- Frankfurt a race in 2014

- 11hrs
- Swim 1hr 15
- Bike 5hrs 30
- Run 4hrs 5m
- Transition 10mins

- 85 kilos.... now
- Ideal weight to reach full potential 75/76 ?
- 80 kilos.... for Frankfurt

- Triathletes more weighty than marathon runners.....

- Each call.....
- Strength to weight ratio improves....

- Faster runner.....

- 50% advice on nutrition....
- Keeping track... What to cut back and what eat more of ?

Frankfurt goal time 2014
Swim 1hr 10m
Bike -5hrs-5hr 20m (zips)
Run 3hr 45m (3hr 30)
Transition 6m
9hr 46-10hr 21m.

Frankfurt
Swim 1hr 10m
Bike 5hrs 10m
Run 3hrs 34m
Transitions 6m
10hrs

I was to have 1 call with Dave that was free at the end of 2013 and 3 more calls 3 calls 30 minutes each (although he allowed the interview to go on for an hour at no extra cost) with Dave throughout 2014. I paid $300 for 90 minutes for those. Two of those were about my specific training for Ironman Frankfurt and one of those was an extended interview that I gave him and he was happy for me to record.

I knew I was over doing it with the consultancy calls as Nick was a great coach and had been participating in Triathlon since 1984 himself. Coincidentally it was after seeing Dave give a talk in England that Nick decided to go into triathlon.

Nick was very open to other people becoming involved and throughout we would discuss what other people chipped in and then decide between us what to try and whether to alter any training slightly or not.

For example when I said I wanted to strengthen my core Nick suggested doing some gym work from October through to December and easing off the bike a little bit.

When Harry suggested the key swimming drill was to swim with one arm and learn to pull more water then Nick adapted and put that into my warm up routines. There were a few other technicalities on my stroke that Harry would pick up on as we were to have 2 more lessons prior to Frankfurt and Nick adapted my drills and swim reps accordingly whilst staying true to his own way of doing it. This kept me interested and I saw my swim improve slowly but steadily in time for Frankfurt.

I really did want to interview Dave however as I was very keen in setting up a new triathlon business as I was not sure how my publishing social enterprise Chipmunkapublishing would do in the future. Better to not have all ones eggs in one basket they say.

Rachel Joyce as Consultant

I had initially agreed to have a monthly call with Rachel right up until the Frankfurt Ironman in July 2014. We had 3 or 4 calls, which went really well. I was aware that she might not want to give too much information away as of course she is still a professional athlete. Not that I would be sharing the calls as they were about my training but that did hold me back with some of my questions. It was fascinating to hear how she focused while she was racing. I was planning on taking a couple of weeks off at Christmas like I did prior to my first Ironman. Rachel warned me against that by saying "I wouldn't". So I got some more base in including some long runs during Christmas and the New Year. I went to Spain with my family for several days and ran every day apart from one when my cold was so bad that I could not face running another half marathon the day after doing another half marathon.

Rachel recommended having a bike fitting. I spoke to the guy she recommended on the phone and he said it was £300. That's when I said to myself I just do not want to pay that. Nick said my position was 95% right anyway so don't bother.

My Ironman expenses were mounting up. You really do have to be able to afford to take up the sport. I was spending quite a bit of money. A monthly amount to Nick, all the kit, race entries, accommodation, vitamins, coconut milk and I had just treated myself to a new bike that Nick helped me get off his friend at a discount. It was a specialized shiv time trial bike. Pretty nifty. I even took the plunge and got myself some zip tubs. The bike was £2500 reduced to around £1800 and the wheels were reduced from £1500 to around £1050.

I decided to splash out a bit until Frankfurt and really planned to cut my spending after then and cut back and make do with what I had. There is only so much I can spend on anything without the feeling that I need to look after the future of my children, family and save for what I hope is the inevitably of old age.

After around 3 calls with Rachel she did not reply over the Christmas period. I'd already paid for the call £100 and did not have it. She apologized a few weeks later saying it was not good enough. Fair enough. We agreed to stop there and have one more call. I imagine she had had such a hard season that she just wanted to forget about Ironman and rightly so. I did not want to interfere in any pros potential to be the athlete they could be.

For me I needed someone I could rely on to be there and that was Nick. He lived just round the corner and was always there.

Achilles Injury – Nick saves the day

Everyone new to Triathlon 'over thinks' it in my opinion. It just such an exciting sport and three sports to learn that its easy to get over excited. My winter training was going great and then with my own stupidity I picked up an injury.

Run Reps with Nick

In January I took the plunge to start doing run reps regularly with Nick. Although looking at my Ironman notes from the year when putting this book together I realized for the first time that I actually did them was in November 2013. It was on 20th November 2013. They were 2 x 2 mile reps first time heart rate below 180. 6m 49 6m 49 6m 51 6m 47sec.1 minute rest in between.

It was so hard that I did not do them every week until January, that says it all! Its one thing running but running to get quicker is harder for sure.

This was harder running than I was doing on my own. I was doing 2-3 runs a week. Usually a long run on my own on a Sunday of around 2 hours, a short quick run of around 40 minutes or a 1-hour medium paced run.

Now it was time to step it up. For many years Nick has been running every Wednesday in Dulwich Park at around 1.45pm with friends. Just go to the park and look for the fastest runner and the fittest looking bloke there and it will be Nick!

My run had let me down in Austria so who better to run with than Nick. Let me explain his running background a bit. He has completed the London marathon 22 times. With a best time of 2hrs 25 minutes and a worst time of 2 hrs 49 minutes. This means he is in the top 250 competitors every time. When he moved over from running to Ironman he was obviously pretty good at the Ironman run as well once he had got his bike mileage up and he was already a good swimmer.

The run reps would go like this. Warm up for around 2 laps of the park – that's around 2 miles. Then 4 sprints of around 40 paces with 40 paces recovery in between to warm up the rest of the body. Then do the reps. each week the reps would differ slightly depending on whether I was on an easy, medium or hard weeks training. The reps would either be in kilometres or miles. Usually it would be kilometres for around 6 weeks and then switch to miles nearer longer races.

The kilometer reps would mean for me running at 3m 30, 3m 40 or 3m 50 second pace and then jogging 3-4 minutes slowly back into the same rep. So ideally no stopping in between. When I first started I would have to stand still for 20 seconds after the first rep but after a few months I could stand still for 4 or 5 seconds and then get back into a slow jog.

The aim was to hit every rep with the same time. For the first couple of months I was going to fast in the early reps and then blowing up by the end.

What I noticed more than anything was how much it hurt compared to jogging. As Ronnie O Sullivan says in his autobiography I run I do not jog. He can run a 34 minute 10km which is quicker than me so fair play although he has not run long distance yet which is another mind game in itself as the longer you go the harder it becomes.

However one thing that running at this pace did for me was make it hurt more. Of course you get out of breath more, which is actually probably the easiest bit to get used to. My stomach hurt a lot more and always done running quicker for a sustained period. How fast you go really does depend on how much pain you want to go through assuming you are doing the correct type of training. Then the other pain is in my bottom. No other way to explain that really. Running really fast does make your bottom hurt and does make you much more likely to want to go to toilet and I do not mean a wee.

Many a time during the run reps especially in the beginning I would have to disappear say 2 or 3 of the 4 reps in to go to the toilet. Occasionally I would even have to slow down during the rep to avoid going to toilet in my pants. No other way to say that either I am afraid.

As course as time goes on and you get more experienced you learn to understand your body better. The more experienced I have become as a runner the longer I leave eating before I run. When I first started I used to not eat 30 minutes or 1 hour before but then you feel the food in your throat. Leave it a bit longer and you can still feel the food in your stomach. Now I will either run first thing in the morning on an empty stomach after a coffee or eat at least 2 and ideally 3 hours or even 3 and a half hours before I run.

Even harder than the kilometer reps were the mile reps. One kilometer is 0.62 of a mile. That last 0.38 of a kilometer you can really feel. The way we did the run reps round Dulwich Park you start off a bit uphill for the first 0.2 km then the next 0.4 km is slightly down a slope so you finish the 1km strong. The rest of the distance to the mile is then a little bit more down the slope but then back up the slope for the last 0.2km when you are at your most fatigued.

When we did the run reps. We would do 3,4 or 5 x 1mile reps or 2,3 or 4 x 2 miles reps. The same 2 mile warm up every time and a 1 or 2 mile warm down. Then my times were at 6m 10 – 6m 40 pace. You finish the rep and then stop for no more than 1 minute to get your heart rate down and then you are off again.

The first one is always tough as you are a bit stiff still. Even though we do 4-6 running sets to waken up the quicker fibre muscles. Each stride contains running about 40 paces at 7/10 effort of pace increasing to 8/10 effort of pace by the last stride. This leaves you feeling pretty bouncy at the start.

The second rep is usually the easiest although still harder than any running I do on any other day (apart from maybe the final 10 minutes of a half marathon if I am on just coffee before and no gels) as you are warmed up and lose but not yet fatigued. The last one is always a killer !

The run reps were making me quicker. When I started off doing the mile reps I could do one at 5m 49, second at 6m 14 and the third at 6m 45seconds. That was totally not how to do it as Nick told me whilst I was doing it but I wanted to see how fast I could do.

After 4 months doing run reps every week I got very consistent and got to understand my body much better. Within 6 weeks before Ironman Frankfurt I could hold 6m 15 second pace exactly for 5 x 1 miles which was a big improvement.

Doing the run reps was a real inspiration for me throughout the whole season. Soon I could show what I was made of at my second attempt at the Spring Ballbuster but first I had to get back out on the bike and get off the turbo and pick up my bike skills again. It was time for my first Sportive.

Hell of the Ashdown 110km of Hills

This event took place on Sunday 24th of February 2013. Good job it was just cycling as I had started to have terrible running pain which stopped me doing a couple of long runs and I had to do 10 days with no running whatsoever. Basically I had gone and bought a pair of Asics without consulting Nick and the heels turned out to be way too high. Combining that with an extra training load and a slightly more aggressive cleat position to get more power on the bike and it led to an overuse injury on my Achilles. Nick saved the day with some timely coaching interventions. More of that later but first let me tell you about my first ever sportive.

It was a great focus for me to enter the Hell of The Ashdown as soon as entries were available not just because it sells it really quickly but it gave me a full plan all of my race were every day until Frankfurt. In fact in order to get my life as organized as possible I had asked Nick to set my sessions all the way from 1st of January right through until Ironman Frankfurt. This was really useful as it helped me plan my life around Ironman or Ironman around my life whichever way you look at it. It meant I could plan for important meetings, family time, holidays etc. knowing that I still had a plan. As I was in my second year of training I was a little more confident in my sessions but having them lined out did make it easier. Of course, they might have to change slightly from time to time depending on whether I achieved them 100%, how my body was feeling etc.... But I would say that I did 90% of the sessions that were set me from January right through until Frankfurt. Occasionally I might skip one through physical or mental fatigue or just not fitting it in or even illness but most of the time I did them.

Entering the Ashdown helped me focus on my turbo. I was determined to not go out on my bike during November, December, January and most of February. I know most triathletes would not do that but we all make our own choices and here is why I chose to do this. One I just felt safer knowing that I was not going out on the roads as much. I like cycling and it's my stronger of the three disciplines but you cannot escape that it is dangerous. Even if you ride beautifully a truck could still hit you or a car god forbid I hope nobody does but the reality is it's dangerous. Also during the winter weather it can get wet, windy, icy and darker so again it is even more dangerous in the winter.

Thirdly I am not very handy doing maintenance so the last thing I wanted was a puncture or bike problem and to be stuck out in the cold. Fourthly by knowing I was just doing turbo sessions for a few months it made me more likely to do the sessions. Sure, its pretty monotonous but it took me less time, as I did not have to take the bike out on the road. I could also watch Seminars, Study Sales and marketing videos for my business and watch inspirational Ironman races to keep me going. Also, on a turbo you do not get a break. You always have to keep peddling so it does make you strong. Sure its not very good for your road skills and Nick did advise me to go out on the bike during the winter but when I said I wanted to stay indoors he made the training schedule around what I wanted as an athlete. I figured I could catch up with my bike handling skills and the Ashdown was the first test in doing that.

The 110km ride is very hilly 2000 metres of climbing. A lot more climbing than I would be doing in Frankfurt so I really good work out to start the season and the countdown.

I drove up there in my car at a reasonable hour. My start was around 9.30am. Every 2 minutes people would go off in groups of 10 or so. I arrived even earlier than I expected so joined a group that had a few people who did not turned up so started about 9.16 am. I was surprised how many people were there. There were hundreds of people who had entered.

Right from the start you turn left and then what starts off flat turns into a big hill. I was in completely in the wrong gear and my chain fell off. I lost my group and was on my own. Not a great start. I actually found it quite amusing a couple of minutes after I had put my chain back on and started riding.

I had loaded up my bike with a few gels taped to the frame of my bike and I had 2 drinks bottles filled with a new drink Nick had told me to start using.
High 5 Energy Source Summer Fruits Flavour. I was in good shape. I had missed a few running sessions and did extra bike sessions instead. Fortunately pedalling the bike had no strain on my Achilles at all.

I soon caught up loads of riders but took it really cautiously for the first 45 minutes or so. We had been told that several riders had fallen off earlier in the morning, as the road had been icy. In fact it had been so icy that they changed the route slightly. Mind you it was getting warmer and what ice there was, had either melted already or was about to. I was not used to riding so close to so many people either. I had to be really careful on the downhill's as I am taller and heavier than most people. I catch them on the downhill even if I don't plan on doing so and the last thing I wanted to do was play around too much with my brakes. I would go past people when it was safe to do but was riding very hesitantly. Then an hour or so into it I really started to enjoy it. The road was no longer wet from the ice, the sun was shining and I felt like I had chosen the right clothes. February is pretty cold of course. I had some long trousers on for the first time and some extra covers on my shoes thank god it was freezing when we started. I also had running gloves on which stopped my fingers getting cold and had a pretty good grip. I had a couple of layers underneath and a thin but warm jacket on.

I remember chatting to one guy who was training for his first Ironman after watching his dad do Ironman Wales. We spoke on and off for about half an hour and then we lost each other. Then a few minutes later I started talking to him again and he looked at me saying I have no idea what you are talking about mate. We'd still basically lost each other and I had found someone else with a red bike and red jacket on i.e. somebody completely different and then I had carried on the conversation I had been having previously. Once the embarrassment was over and I gave an apology I decided to push on.

The Sportive was thinning out a bit as it went on as people set in at their own pace. However at one stage there was quite a big group from Penge cycling club of about 10 riders or so that were really getting in the way. I was basically quicker than all of them when it was straight but would then have to be really careful going round corners as they went really wide round the corners. So I would go all the way to the back and then try and get up tot the front again. Eventually I had to push pretty hard to get in front of them and leave them behind. I just didn't feel safe riding anywhere near that lot.

Thank god I do not ride with a cycling club I thought. Although Nick and others were suggesting I should to pick up my handling skills. It was just not practical for me. It would mean interfering with valuable family time as would joining a triathlon club. I did all of my training on my own throughout my first years training apart from a few key sessions with Nick and a B races. I was doing the same in my second year in apart from the run reps which were great but generally enjoyed training on my own as I could train when I want and get it done and then get on with my day and I liked testing myself to see if I could do it. I also liked being in the moment and at one with nature and the elements. Sometimes when swimming I would try and not swim on my own but some people were just too fast to catch their slipstream.

The longer the Sportive went on the more I enjoyed it. They are not races as such as there is no position but everyone gets a time and a certificate at the end. There are allocated stops if you want them. I stopped after a couple of hours left my bike outside, had a quick wee and then grabbed a cake and had a quick cup of tea. As I looked at a couple of hundred people sat down having a chat I thought what am I doing here. I am training for an Ironman. Every second that goes by is a second lost and not me reaching my training potential for my next Ironman Triathlon which was only a few months away.

I went back out there and was then on a mission for the rest of the Ashdown. I knew most of the big hills were coming up and I was ready. Five minutes later I saw the biggest hill I had ever seen. It was so steep. I thought right I will just do a quick cadence. I sat down the whole way and pedalled quickly over taking a couple of people who were lone figures in the distance when I started. That's it I thought. It could not have been as steep as White's hill where Nick had taken me in my first hill test in my first year of training but this looked more intimidating as you could see further in front of you.

I kept going for it and went straight past the next stop, which was around 45 minutes later. Then back in over the finish line. 110km and 2000metres of climbing in the bag for Frankfurt. There was a nice looking finish line with lots of people mingling around it and it felt great to finish. What gave me a lot of confidence was how good I felt at the end. I felt really strong and could have gone on longer. I'd probably eaten and drank too much but felt great. Then I went inside and treated myself to a fantastic fry up and a coffee and received my certificate.

I had got round safely and strongly. It had taken longer than I thought however. 4hrs 25 minutes. I guess its not called Hell of the Ashdown for nothing.

Soon it would be time for me next race my second year at the Spring Ball Buster.

Four months before Ironman Frankfurt, Spring Ballbuster 2 March 2013

It was time for me to participate in my second Spring Ballbuster event. The year before it had been my second ever race. I had been training for triathlon for 8 months and was pretty fit by then but still really a novice. First time around it had taken me 3hrs 46 minutes. My splits were - Run1 1h 1m 30s, transition 1 - 2m 29s, bike 1hr 26m 43s, transition 2 - 2m 16s, Run

2 1hr 13m 22s. I came 186th out of 276 that time. I had looked at the times before and hope to come in the top half. I was not as quick as I thought and had clearly gone too quick on the first run and suffered as a result on the second run. This time around I was hoping to pace the two runs so they were even paced.

I was in good hands. My coach Nick had come as high as 4th overall one time.

My swimming was coming on really well after I had my second lesson with Harry Wiltshire in early February and I had got my 3km swim time down from 68 minutes down to 63 minutes. When I saw Harry he said that he had been looking through some old copies of Triathlon 220 magazine and saw a photo of Nick running on the cover. Nick really was a class runner and class Ironman athlete with loads of experience so I was lucky to be coached by him.

This was a Duathlon of course and had no swim leg. Not even Michael Phelps would be even to swim up Box Hill if it was full of water as its steep! There were 5 laps of the dreaded Box Hill. First an 8-mile run, then 3 x 8 mile bike laps and then the killer second 8-mile run to finish. I heard some cyclists going past during my running part of race who were not in the event say "its hard enough climbing this hill on a bike let alone running up it".

This time I wanted to do a lot better. I had 3 goals - 1 mega goal, a tough goal and a goal that would give me more confidence. I really wanted to get in the top 50, top 100 or at least the top half.

Nick said to just see how I went.

I drove down there nice and early on my own. By now I was experienced enough to know to have breakfast 3 hours before racing. A big bowl of porridge and a strong coffee. I took a coffee flask with me on the way. It was about an hour's journey from my house and I was playing some personal development cd. Probably Anthony Robbins, Jim Rohn, Brian Tray or Earl Schoff. I was one of the first ones there and manage to time my turn at the toilet before it got too busy.

I looked at the start list and saw a name that I recognized from Ironman – Lucy Gossage. Looks like first place was not going to be possible then. I was determined to get a good start. The year before I felt like I was being swallowed up at the start. This time the starting sound went off and we were away. There was a bit of a surprise. I sprinted away and realized that I was in the lead ! In fact I was still in the lead after 5, 10, 15, 20..... wait... seconds that's right... then I thought I better slow down... I looked at my Garmin and I was running under 6 minute mile pace ! I had nearly 16 miles to run and 24 miles to cycle left. I slowed down a bit and then one person went past... then 2.... Then a group of a dozen or so... then nobody for a few seconds and a few more people.... No one else for a few seconds and then a bit more....
My plan had been to around 58 minutes for the first 8 miles so after a quick half a mile at the start I slowed down to make sure I was on the correct pace.

After the first couple of miles I held my position. Catching the odd person up and the odd person coming past. I was really running to my own pace and my own race and just looking in front. I actually felt great. The start was 8 am and it was really cold. After a few miles my head was too hot as I had a woolly hat on so I threw it on top of a bin. I had a long sleeve tight craft top on, triathlon shorts and running gloves. My fingers still felt cold so I think I had the correct kit on. I remember the year before I had a sleeveless top on and was shivering before the start, bitterly cold.

I got through 10km in 44 minutes which was very even paced after the first mile and that was my quickest 10km ever up and down hills. I felt great. I got into the end of the 8 miles in 58 minutes exactly as planned. Nick had said anything under 60 minutes would be good and 58 minutes was ideal.

So far everything was going according to plan. This time my transition was much quicker as I was more experienced, had more confidence in what I was actually going to do and was a fitter and stronger athlete. There were 360 people in the event and I came in 92nd male overall after the first run.

My transition the first year was 2 minutes 29 seconds. This time it was 57 seconds. I moved up from 92nd male to 83rd male in transition. Then it was time for my strength, the bike.

I really went for it on the bike and pushed the whole way round. I had an energy bar at the start (3 or 4 bites at 10-15 minute intervals in the first 45 minutes on the bike) and a gel towards the end and then 1 drinks bottle with carbs in it.

During the bike I overtook quite a few people. I only remember a couple of people going past who were going super quick. It was great going out for my first race on my Specialized Shiv. It was really a TT bike ideal for flatter ground but good to test it on some hilly parts. Nick said it was good to test my handling skills and good strength work out using that bike instead of my road bike with TT bars on it.

I remember getting completely the wrong gear on the first 2 laps thinking I had reached the top of the hill where you see the crowd and then turning a corner to almost come to a stop. Each time several people overtook me but then when I got back into the right gear on a bit of a flattish downhill bit I was able to go straight past all of them again. On the third lap I chose the correct gear at the correct time and overtook several people at the same point without getting overtaken first.

So my bike split in my first Spring Ballbuster had been 1hr 26m 43s. This time it was much better. 1hr 20m 55 seconds. I had moved up from 83rd to 62nd overall from the end of Transition 1 to the end of the bike leg. How would my second transition compare to the first year I did it ? My transition 2 improved from 2m 16s to 1m 08s and took me to 60th overall.

I knew I was going quicker this time around. Of course I did not know exactly how much quicker at the time. I was in the moment and enjoying competing.

How was I going to do on the second run this time around? In my first Spring Ballbuster I really suffered on the second run. This time I didn't feel great but better than I did the first year.

I was a year stronger, had a years more training in the bag and was more confident. This time I just had one gel on me as I had just finished in the last 2 minutes of the bike leg. I knew that would last half an hour and then was planning on using my last gel 30 minutes into the second run.

One guy moved ahead of me at the start of the run. He was going really quickly. Straight away I was finding it harder than the first run and doubted that I would be able to do 58 minutes again.

The previous year I had fallen apart somewhat by going from 1hr 1 minute on the first run to 1hr 13 minutes on the second run. This time I knew I was going to do better than the second run the year before but only time would tell how much better.

Instead of running 7 minute miles they were nearer 8 minute miles but I still felt ok. No stomach issues, tired legs but still flexible and still running. I took my gel exactly on 30 minutes and just went for it as best as I could.

I got to the last mile and thought I would really give it a push with about two thirds of a mile to go. Just before that I had to stop for a moment as I had been running with a shoelace undone for over a mile. I was near the top of the hill by now and really went for it. Uh oh. My left hamstring completely seized up and I had to stop. I think it was a combination of stopping and tying up my shoelace a minute or so before and then running as fast as I could again.

Then I decided to do what I saw Craig Alexander do once when he was winning Kona when he stretched his. Oh no. That made it feel even worse. I only stopped for about 5 or 6 seconds as I had less than a mile to go. I managed to get into a rhythm and although I was now running 9 minute mile pace I could keep going by running shorter stride and putting more weight on my right leg whilst really running on my toes even more on both legs.

I was relieved to still be able to run until the end. It only cost me 1 or 2 places at most as people were pretty spaced out anyway. Then I could hear and see the finish. There were people cheering. It felt great. I got to where I thought the finish was and heard some guy say well done, mate. They cannot catch you now. You've made it. Then I realized the finish line was actually another metre to the left. Two guys were sprinting as fast as they could. By the time I realized and started to run again one of them overtook me but I stayed in front of the other one.

I said well done to the guy who just overtook me. I had my Ironman Frankfurt cap on. I was so obsessed with the race that I had not yet participated in that I wore the official Ironman Frankfurt hat from the previous years race on every training run that I did. This was a kind of future visualization for me. I had done the same thing before Austria wearing an Ironman Austria visor during every run. Theses little gimmicks were that kind of thing that made me want to train and more me keep on running during the hard moments training.

The guy said Ironman. That's cool. I just did my first Half a few weeks ago and have my first one this year coming up. We spoke for 5 minutes of so munching at rehydrating at the finish line the freebies, which included some 3 bottles of lovely coconut water for me. We wished each other good luck and went our separate ways.

I was on a real adrenaline high after finishing. My 2nd run split the year before had been 1hr 13 minutes. This time it was 1hr and 4 minutes 46s. I was 78th male over and 86th overall out of 276 finishers.

So I had improved from 186th out of 276 to 86th out of 270 finishers in 12 months. One hundred places better than the year before. My time had also improved a great deal from 3hrs 46 minutes the first year to 3hrs 24 minutes this time. So 22 minutes quicker than the year before.

This time I took my bike to the car, got changed and then walked around a bit to stop me getting too stiff before I sat down and watched people coming over the finish line. My recovery was much quicker this year as well.

I managed to catch the awards presentation. The overall winner was a woman for the first time – Lucy Gossage. She didn't receive any money for winning or even a trophy that I noticed but lots of free gels! I spoke to her afterwards and said her name was familiar and that I was doing my second Ironman in 4 months time. She said Ironman was her sport and she loved it. I said I would like to interview her and would pay her. This was not a planned moment. I was on a high after doing quite well in my own race as she Lucy was as well and she was very pleased to be offer money for an interview. You may not be aware but the life on Ironman professional is very tough with very low prize money for such brilliant and dedicated sportsmen if you compare them to tennis players, footballers or golfers for example.

It was a perfect end to another great Ironman preparation day for Ironman Frankfurt.

Soon I was going to have fun doing my first ever half marathon race and that was only 13 days later.

Fleet Half Marathon 16 March 2014

Next it was my first ever half marathon race. The day before the race and the morning of the race was particularly stress free. I was used to having to get al my Triathlon or Duathlon kit ready and then tidy up the car, adjust the seats and put my bike in. This time I just had to take my running kit and make sure I turned up at the start line ready to go. I could also wear a pair of shorts instead of Triathlon shorts, which were more comfortable and looked less ridiculous. I insisted on wearing my Ironman visor though. Anything to make me feel stronger and keep me finished for Frankfurt.

Up until then the fastest time I had ran a half marathon in training was around 1 hour 53 minutes. Of course that is not how you run fast. I knew I was going to run a lot faster but how quick depended on how well I paced it and how much pain I was willing to go through.
I had been doing run reps since November and hardly missed a week since January.

Nick said that by doing run reps you could get your body used to running faster so that you could run a minute slower in an Ironman and find it a lot easier than you would do otherwise. Of course the half marathon was only a B race for me so I wanted to do well. I remember before I started doing them thinking that I could do 1hr 45 minutes if I really pushed it. A few weeks in and training was going well and Nick was chatting with myself and Jim asking how fast do you think Jason can do a half marathon in Jim if he does the reps. Jim said 1 hour 30 minutes. Wow. That was a lot quicker than I was thinking. That really motivated me and made me want to keep going. Then Nick said yes with another year's reps after that you should be able to get down to 1hr 25 minutes if you pace yourself right and put in the work. Oh my god. That was quick.

The reps were going well. They were extremely varied. For example here are 2 from the last 2 weeks in January 2014.

Week starting Jan 20th - Wed run reps 3 x1 mile. 6m 13, 6m 13, 6m 10.

Week starting 27th Jan - 4 x 2 miles. 7m 4 sec, 7m

5sec, 7m 8sec, 7m 8sec, 7m 8sec, 7m 7sec, 7m 7s, 6m 48 seconds. Jim said to sprint the last 300 metres so i did.

Here I'd like to tell you a bit more about Jim. Jim was Nick's friend from Blackheath Harriers. They had been running together on and off for 20 years. Jim was now 65 years old and competing for Great Britain at his age group in Olympic distance triathlons. He has run multiple marathons with a best time around 2hrs 45 minutes. His best distance was shorter distances 1 mile and 5km and he'd done his first Ironman at the age of 40 and done 5 Ironman's all together with a best time of 10hrs 52 minutes.

Combine that with Nick who has ran the marathon 22 times all under 2 hrs 49 minutes and competed in over 30 Ironman's and was still doing them in 9 hrs 30 minutes at the age of 54 and I was running with some talented runners with fantastic experience. I just did what they said as best as I could.

Anyway, time for the race. I was really excited. I got there early. There were 2500 people running. The weather was fairly nice. The start was at 10,30 am. In fact it turned out to be the hottest day of the year by far and the first hot and sunny day of the year. I did some pretty intense warming up five minutes before the start. I think I probably over did it a bit.

Then you could choose where you wanted to go for the start. You could stand in the 3 hr. section, 2hr 45minutes section down to the 1hr 30-minute section, 1 hour 15 minute section and then in front of that. I thought I might as well go right to the front. Nobody seemed to mind. A couple of minutes before the start someone asked me to take a photo of them and their charity.

Everyone at the front was pretty serious. There were some pretty muscly blokes there. A few with army t-shirts on looked very strong and quick. There was a tape in front of us. There was a count down at 1 minute and then from 30 seconds. With about 30 seconds to go one of the starters looked at me and said you look terrified. I was definitely pumped up. 3,2,1 go... I sped off quickly trying to avoid clashing with other runners. It was about 150 metres straight ahead and then a sharp left up a gradual slope that went on for a third of a mile or so then the rest of the course was pretty flat, only rolling slights in a few places.

Back to the start... There I was 5 seconds in and... I am in the lead... 10 seconds gone I am still in the lead of 25000 runners... Where is everyone I am thinking... I turn round the corner and I am still in front... I look at me Garmin and its 5-minute mile pace... I better slow down... then a couple of seconds later some army guy runs past me... Then another guy runs past (he turns out to be the eventual winner – not me - as I recognize him on the website a few days later). Then, a few seconds later 1,2,3,4, a dozen people run past me... Every few seconds more and more people run past me... but less than before... then a minute goes by and a few more people go past...

By half a mile I am into a nice rhythm and conscious of slowing down so I can save myself. The first mile and a half are at my predicted pace for a 1 hr. 30 marathon. Then as each mile goes past I find it harder to maintain the pace... and drop back a bit until I am running 7 minutes 15 second pace... It's also surprisingly hot. There is great support throughout big parts of the course as Fleet is quite a busy place. The best moments are when we run through the town centre and there are thousands of people watching, stood up, by café's outside pubs etc., standing outside the shops and on the high street. The event has been run for many years and the local people and family members and friends of the runners give you a real boost. I drop down to 7 minute 30 second mile pace... I have one really bad mile about mile 8-9 which seems a bit up hill and then I get over it once I have some electrolytes and pour some water over my head at the aid station. I also consciously run in the shade for a bit which is a big help... Pretty soon we pick it up for the finish. My last 0.12 miles is my quickest of the race and there I am across the finish line extremely please to come in at 1 hr. 36 minutes and 59 seconds. Considering I had gone out way to quick and that it was really hot I was very pleased with the result. Not a 1hr 30 half marathon but I could dream on for another day.

My final position was 409th out of 2445. Almost a year before it had taken me 3 hrs 15 minutes to run 21 miles at Cranham and the major difference apart from being another year into the sport and being stronger and fitter doing the run reps which gave me some speed instead of being a one paced jogger.

Next it was the time of year to bring the time trials in and build up the volume on the bike. First I'd like to mention how I avoided a serious injury that would have blown my chances of competing in Ironman Frankfurt

Running Injury – Nick saved the day !!

I naively decided to buy a new pair of Asics without consulting Nick. I had the Asics Oberon I forget the exact model number and they were a shoe I felt good in, nice and cushioned .... I decided to just buy the latest version...... Of course each edition of shoe changes in different ways whilst ones feet remain the same size and shape.

I didn't think anything of it until every time I started to run I was in agony. In fact on my long Sunday run in January it hurt so much that I had to finish 15 minutes early. It was really bizarre. It would be fine... then it would hurt like hell for 20 minutes or so and then just as I was about to stop it would go away... It got even worse doing the run reps one week and I mentioned it to Nick.

Nick said it was my Achilles and told me I needed to rest from running and recommended I go and see his Physiotherapist. Paul O Hara whose company is called Back On Track.

I booked the physio for only a few days later. When I saw him he gave the following diagnosis.

You have an Achilles injury. It's a 1 ½ out of 10 seriousness. It's a good job you came to see me when you did or it would have got worse. He showed me some strengthening exercises.

The physio said that 3 things combined to give me the injury. He said that the increase in training, the new cleat position on my bike which I had ask Nick to help me get more power on the Bike and he had moved my left cleat slightly forward and the change in trainers with higher heels put too much pressure on the Achilles.

Nick decided to put the cleat position back, stopped me running for 10 days and helped me choose some new lighter Asics with lower heels as the one I had been using previously were no longer available. I had just bought 3 new pairs of trainers costing £270. Nick said that he used to cut the heels of his trainers. He said it doesn't look great but its fine for running. So he introduced me to this guy in Beckenham who cut all 3 pairs for £22.50. That saved me some money there.

This made me realise that I was grateful to have a coach. I'd only thought I could do an Ironman in the first place if I got Nick to coach me as I knew nothing about swimming, cycling or running before I met Nick. I knew more about playing Rugby, Football, Cricket and different martial arts.

What a relief.
I'd only missed 10 days running altogether and did an extra couple of bike sessions instead and a longer swim. The physio showed me the strengthening exercise, said I had good biomechanics and told me not to come back. Job done. Nick had intervened crucially at the right time to keep my Ironman Frankfurt 2014 dream alive.

Whatsmore in between this pain which lasted a few weeks I had ran my 2 fastest long distance runs ever at the Ballbuster and Fleet and was looking good for Frankfurt.

Turning Time Trial Races into Brick Sessions

Could I keep up the training with some more B races and Time Trials.

The year before I had done 2 x 25 time trials, 1 x 50 mile time trial all with 30-40 minute run sessions straight after i.e. turning them into brick sessions. This season I was going to turn up the training volume a little by doing the following distances 5 weekends in a row 2 x 25 miles, 2 x 50 miles and 1 x 100 miles.

First up it was the Addiscombe 25 mile time trial on Sunday the 27th of April. The year before it had been my first time trial and it had taken me 1hr 12 minutes. It had gone ok except when falling off the bike when at a standstill trying to take a drink in going up a slope in to steep a gear. This time around it started well for the first mile until I saw a Marshall at a roundabout that pointed where to go. I thought it was straight on continuing down the dual carriageway. He seemed to be pointing to the left however so I turned left. Pretty soon I thought I must be going the wrong way.

After about a minute or so it just looked too slow to be a time trial. Then there was a big hill. I climbed up it for about 20 seconds and then realized I must be going the wrong way. I turned back round got back on the roundabout where I was before and saw the Marshall.

"Is it straight on here mate? I think I went the wrong way".

He said, "I tried to tell you it was straight on".

I was not that bothered. I just thought, well that was an extra couple of miles speed training. The rest of the time trial went ok as did the run that Nick had set me straight afterwards. My legs felt surprisingly springy during my short run afterwards. I saw my time and I was embarrassed. It was about 1hr 9 minutes My Garmin said I had gone nearly 27 miles. I was have been in the last 2 or 3 places with my actual time. I had gone the correct way I would have jumped up another 20 or so places so I asked them to disqualify me.

I used my TT bike. I was surprised how it was not that much quicker than my results the previous year. The specialized Shiv with its aero wheels was not that much quicker than my Felt bike and I was meant to be fitter. Maybe it was windy this year. I'd know more as I did more Time trials over the coming weeks.

I had another 25-mile time trial the following week so would pay more attention to the actual course that time. Next up was the Wigmore 25 miler on May 4th 2014.

I got there early and this time managed to stay on course. I finished with a time of 1hr 5 minutes and 3 seconds. Just over 1 minute quicker than my personal best time for 25 miles which was set on the same course the previous year. I came 62nd out of 113 finishers, which was very good for me in a time trial. I also won a cheque for £10 for being the nearest to 1hr 5 minutes. My first prize as a triathlete. It made me smile. It had covered my entry fee and left me with £2 profit but then you add petrol and drinks and then that would soon be eaten up.

Wow, just 1 minute quicker with an extra years training and my aero bike and zipp wheels. Cycling is a tough sport. Still I was very pleased with a PB. It might be that a sub 1hr time trial was just a dream to big for me at the age of 39. Who knows how long I would stay in the sport? Anyway I had bigger goals to complete my second full distance Ironman and get a personal best in that.

Next up was my first 50-mile time Trial of the season. The Norlond 50 mile TT combine. I was looking forward to it. The run had felt good after my time trial the previous week as well so I was expecting a good ride.

I got there nice and early. In fact I got to every time trial nice and early so I could relax and get ready. What I always found the most difficult and the most stressful was finding the start line. I always asked the organizer and then asked one of the numbers going before me where the start was. They would say its straight on here, left there etc.... and I would always get lost... I would always try and follow someone down to the start but half of the time they would ride so quickly that I would not see them again. This is exactly what happened on the morning of May 11th at the Norlond 50mile TT combine.

By the time I had found the start I had been riding for 30 minutes, stopping once or twice and then going as hard as I could for 4-5 miles realizing I had been going the wrong way. By the time I found the start was racing for 7-8 miles before the start and then had a 3-minute penalty for missing my start time! Oh dear, well extra bike training I suppose and a mental test. Also I was pretty confident that even I could not get lost on an Ironman bike leg but only time would tell.

By the time I got to the start I only had to wait 2 minutes for a space as someone did not turn up. That was lucky or my penalty would have been much more than 3 minutes. I eventually finished in 2 hrs 18 minutes and 51 seconds, which was 32nd out of 40 overall. My actual time had been 2 hrs 15 minutes and 51 seconds. My actual time would have only moved me up to 30th place such is the competition at these events. Again the run afterwards went fine.

The tea and cakes always go down great after I get back in from the run after a time trial as well. I always noticed that everyone else there seemed super skinny. I had a brief chat to some guy who had overtaken me in this race and the race the previous week. He had just got back from cycling across America in a Cycling race. He said he was the first Britain to ever complete the race. When he burnt passed me at around 30 miles an hour the previous week he said keep going, which was nice. Pretty soon after that he just rode off into the distance and next time I saw him was having a cup of tea and a biscuit. He was the only guy there who wasn't skinny. He had massive muscly legs.

Next up was the San Fairy Ann cc 50m-time trial. It is described as a lumpy course on the club's website. I was pleased with the work out and went round in a time of 2 hrs 17 minutes and 48 seconds. My position was 26th out of 41 finishers. The winner finished in 1hr 51 minutes and four people went under 2 hrs.

I thought that on a flat course I was capable of 2 hrs 11 so on a lumpy course I was quite happy with that. The run afterwards went great as well. I felt really confident going into my first ever 100-mile time trial the following week.

I was more nervous going into the Hounslow and District Wheelers the following Sunday 25th of May2014. The first starter was at 8.00am and I was on just after 9.00am.

I was aiming for a total time of 4hrs 35 minutes. I had the drinks system on my Specialized Shiv, which consists of a whole in the stem where you fit a drinks bag. I had been using it for the other time trials so I was getting used to it by now. I had only one other drinks bottle on my bike. I also had 1 or 2 energy bars and 3 gels to consume during the ride.

I managed to find the start easily enough this time. Thank god. You do not want to be wasting too much energy before a 100 mile Time Trial followed by yet another run. Before the start I was shivering. It was sunny but absolutely freezing. The weather forecast was for a hot morning later on. Some guy was wrapping people in blankets giving people a massage before they started. He could see me shivering so helped me out and put a blanket on me for 30 seconds and rubbed my shoulders. Then I was 1 minute from the start and ready for the off. One thing I liked about this course was that it was pretty flat and consisted of 10 x 10 mile laps. I figured that even I with my appalling sense of direction could not get lost on this route and... i was... to be grateful... correct... This time I navigated my way round... By the third lap I learnt to pace the course much better... I also liked the idea that if I had a mechanical issue and had to retire that I would not be stuck 30 or 50 miles from where I had started which would be the case if I was in a 2 or 3 lap race.

I made sure I had some money and my mobile phone on me just in case anything went wrong. I usually did this for my time trials and had been lucky not to have any mechanical issues such as punctures or anything else going wrong with my bike. The only problem I really had been getting lost and not being as fast as I wanted to be.

This time things were going well. I even managed to over take a couple of people during the first 25 miles. Then the inevitable super riders going past more frequently than me overtaking people with quicker cadence and bigger gears ! Most of the people I did overtake seemed to be about 70 years old ! So much for my World Championship Kona dreams. Time for a change of career maybe.

I was just going up to 25 miles when I went for a drink and there was none left in my straw. Uh oh. Had I been drinking too quickly ? I got through 25 miles at 1hr 5 minutes, which I was pleased with and felt great. I was bursting for the toilet as I had been rehydrating a lot before the race. I want to make sure I did not bonk during the race.

I stopped for the loo behind a bush for about 1 minute and decided to check my Shiv bag. Yes it was empty. So it was working but I had just drank very quickly. I got back into a rhythm and then got through 50 miles in 2hrs 15 minutes.

The weather had started off cloudy for the first 30 minutes then it was sunny all the way. This was nice at the start but then as the race went on I started to feel hotter and hotter. I had my first energy bar during the first hour with a nibble every 10 minutes or so then the plan was to sip on drink and take one gel an hour for hours 2,3 and 4. By the 4th hour I was really starting to get tired. I had an extra energy bar, which I had not planned on taking but it really helped me out in the last 20 miles. I ran out of liquids by 45 miles and the gels started to taste horrible. Whatsmore I could see other people stopping every now and then and having bottles given to them by their friends and partners. I had travelled on my own. What I should have done was asked for some water from somewhere or even put extra drink bottles somewhere along the route, which is what I heard other people did.

I did feel unusually hot. First I thought it was definitely lack of fluid. I got to the finish and was delighted to end in 4hrs and 45 minutes. That was a respectable time for me. I was not looking forward to the run. I had some much needed fluid before I went for my run. My transition was a bit slow. There was a bit of a steep ride up hill back to the start but only a mile and a bit and then I put the bike in the car and got changed.

I was not looking forward to the run. My legs felt like jelly not as good as after the other races. I had ridden a lot further and it had been later in the day and the temperature hotter. Then I realized what was wrong.

The back of my knees and calves were bright red. I had sunburn! I managed to do the run but cut it short and ran for about 20 minutes (instead of the planned 30 minutes) a minute slower per mile than I had planned.

I was delighted to get back in and eat well before setting out and going home. I'd learnt a lot that day.

I'd come 78th out of 102 finishers. Twenty people did not finish. They'd either given up, had a mechanical or crashed. I was grateful that neither of those three had happened to me. I saw an ambulance with one guy lying on the floor on the road. He must have had a bad crash, as he was not moving at all.

Now Ironman Frankfurt – The European Championships was only 6 weeks to the day. My next test would be 3 weeks before Frankfurt – The toughest 70.3 course in the world as World Champion Chris McCormack once called it Ironman Uk 70.3 Wimblewall.

First I want to tell you about the other Ironman Professionals that I interviewed on the phone and how that shaped my approach to training and racing.

Interviewing the Ironman Professionals

Having spoken to Dave Scott and Rachel Joyce I decided I really wanted to interview more people. I contacted quite a few professionals. Some responded and some didn't.

I interviewed Leanda Cave, which was fantastic. She is the only woman to have won the World Championship at all 3 distances. That's Olympic distance, Half Ironman and then full Ironman distance. It was fascinating hearing her talk. I was asking her about how she races and what makes her such a winner.

I decided to get in touch with Ironman UK winner Daniel Hawksworth. He was an up and coming pro with a swim background and still quite new to the Sport. Chatting to Dan was really interesting. He was a very pleasant, passionate guy with a lot of interesting information and came across well during the recording.

The Interview with Lucy Gossage went really well as well.

The highlight of the interviews at this stage was interviewing 6 times Ironman World Champion Mark Allen. I figured if I had already spoken to Dave then I must speak to Mark. The call with Mark lasted about 45 minutes and is one of the most inspiring conversations I have ever had. He came across as so calm and focused at the same time. He spoke of the first time he finally beat Dave Scott in 1989 and how we felt like he was shot out of a canon at the last aid station. He also spoke of his last win and how he wanted to give up 1000 times but wanted to carry on 1001 times to win. I'd already heard any interviews I could find on you tube but speaking to him directly and in depth was more personal and had even more of an impact.

I have recorded all these interviews and made them available for you. All you have to do is go to www.141triathlon.com and check out my Long Distance Triathlon website.

Thanks Jim Phelan

Just before I tell you how my Half Ironman and Ironman went and I want to give a big thank you to Jim Phelan. My awesome coach Nick Kinsey was in

Majorca coaching for 3 months from March to May and we kept in touch regularly. Nick gave me a motivational call every week, which really kept me going. As he was away it meant that he could not be with me for the run reps but I made sure I went there every week and every week Jim was there. He would ask me how my training was going every week and he would time his run reps around mine so he would help push me to go faster. Jim is a lovely guy and inspirational to still train so regularly and hard at the age of 65. I've never seen him out of his running gear yet we have spent a lot of time running together. He has shared a lot of his training and racing experience with me over the years and his companionship made me look forward to putting the hard graft in so thanks Jim !

Now it was time for my final warm up race before my much-deserved 3 week taper.

Ironman UK 70.3 Wimblewall June 2014

I'd really been looking forward to doing an official Ironman event in England. I was obsessing about the times and was convinced that I was going to come in the top half and do a lot better than that. Nick said to just relax and execute the race. One piece of advise from Rachel Joyce stuck to my mind. She said to not over do the second half of the run and to save my legs for Frankfurt.

The race was on the Sunday. I drove up on the Saturday morning, leaving the house at 5.00am. It was a very long drive to Exmoor from London. I drove past Stonehenge and stopped at a little chef for a coffee and an extra breakfast. I had decided to drive to the event first and put all my kit in and then drive to the hotel, which was 40 minutes, drive from the event.

Coming in race morning was no problem as I had booked my accommodation with Nirvana Europe and they were driving a minibus to the race, which would let me focus on executing my race plan on the day.

Driving into Exmoor and Wimblewall itself it was beautiful. It was so green and hilly. There was 1200 metres of climbing on the bike course. I was feeling really confident about my swim for once as I had a lesson with Harry Wiltshire the week before at Brockwell Lido and he had actually gone in the pool with me showing me different ways how to draft on the legs and just below the hips, how to sight and how to turn over somebody both ways if people were getting in the way. He also showed my how to turn up and over round the pull buoys so I did not get crushed by other people. These were invaluable tips for someone who was not a great swimmer and was very inexperienced in open water swimming.

Some of the hills were so steep they needed to be seen to be believed. I found it funny seeing them and a relief to know that Frankfurt was a lot flatter overall. It seemed to take forever to set everything up and get registration done, the bike in and then eventually get out of the car park. I was stuck in the car for 30 minutes trying to get out. Eventually I arrived at the hotel around 3,00pm. The race began at 7.00am the next day.

I had an early dinner at around 6.00pm. I was the first one in and the first one out.

Next morning I got down nice and early and had a lovely warm porridge, some scrambled eggs and coffee. I met Eimear Mullen at breakfast who favourite to win the women's race again so that was pretty inspirational.

Everyone else had Ironman tattoos given to him or her by the race organizer. I did not put mine on thinking that I may rub off some of the P20 sun cream that I had put on.

I'd set the alarm for 3.30am and had breakfast by 4.00am.

As we drove off to the race most people were pretty quiet on the mini bus. I spoke to one guy who had done around 20 Ironman's for a bit but all our minds were elsewhere. I had checked out the transition's the day before and the run up from the lake onto the beach into T1. It was quite a long run up the hill.

The swim course still looked long. I was so used to looking at a 50-metre pool that anything longer looked a lot longer.

I went to the front at the swim like I always did. This time when the gun went I was surprised that fewer people were overtaking me than normal. I knew I was going to be quicker than before but not sure how quick I could be. With Harry the previous week I had really improved my 100-metre speed all of a sudden with the drafting. This time I managed to draft properly for the first time ever. I must have been drafting people for nearly half the swim. As I came in after the 1.9km I had taken 37 minutes. That was great for me. I had got nowhere near that time in the pool. I felt like it was going to be a good day.

I even picked up someone else's hat from the floor so now had two hat mementoes for my training. Yes, I wear the Ironman swim hats all the time in the pool just like I do the visors during every run. I should be getting commission... Anyway back to the race...

I knew the bike course was going to be tough. I had my time trial bike, which was going to make the hills even harder than when riding my road bike my Felt. Still I knew I had the legs from the 100-mile time trial that I had done a few weeks before. Not sure that I could hold it all together for the run though. The bike went good. I was in a zone. I was having such fun that I even stopped for the loo after about an hour. I'd taken 2 Dioralyte sachets mixed with water in transition for my salts and had 2 bars and a couple of gels for the bike. I think I used an extra gel later on at the aid station. I remember Tim Don telling me that the bike course was really tough and the pros were all 20 minutes slower on this type of course than in a normal 70.3 so that meant even longer for someone like me.

I got off the bike with 3 hours 15 minutes for the leg. Slower than I though but I felt great and looking at the time I knew if I ran all the way and got my nutrition right going slow through the aid stations that I would go under 6 hours which would be an awesome time for me on such a touch course. It had got really hot on the bike. It had been cloudy for the first 45 minutes on the bike but on the rest of the bike and all the run the sun was shining. The crowd was really good with people supporting most of the run course. The run course was idyllic. It was a combination of pavement, trail and grass. This suited me as most of my runs included the same terrain running from home, around Crystal Palace Park. The run was also very up and down which also suited me as I was used to that. It was definitely a stamina and strength course. I felt like I was more of a stamina athlete than a quick one so embraced that idea.

The only silly thing I did all day was to run out of transition the wrong way at the start of the run. It only cost me about 10 seconds. The reason was that my shades were so dark. Nick figured this out when he took a look at them. It was another piece of kit that I had bought without asking Nick. This was the last time I used them. Looking back I was lucky I had not had an accident on any bike rides as compared to the shades I have now they were like wearing night masks or night goggles. You know what some people wear when they go to sleep on an aeroplane or even at home, as they do not want any light to go in.

The run started well and I knew that if I did not fall apart on it that I would finish in less than 6 hours. I had a great feeling starting the run. It was fantastic to get off the bike, safely knowing that I had no more climbs to ride up and no more cycling to do. Near the start of the run I caught a glimpse of the finish line. I could see the overall time which confirmed that as long as I ran under 2 hours then I would be finishing in under 6 hours which on this tough course felt like a victory. I'd be running long runs most Sundays and had build quite a few half marathon runs in, all of them under 2 hours and that was going at easy pace. I had done most of those runs before breakfast as well. Of course I had not had a swim and a hilly bike ride before but I knew I felt surprisingly flexible and nimble coming off the bike.

On the run and I started to get into a good rhythm. One mile in... feeling good... The euphoria of completing the bike leg starts to wear off... Focus on the crowd and enjoy the atmosphere and check my pace every few seconds on the Garmin... Now keep the rhythm going and look at the Garmin less... Take the nutrition on offer... Carb drink... Isotonic... Nice.. Mile 2... on track... Mile 3... Its sunny than I thought actually... The course is undulating for sure... Off road... nice in the shade... on the grass for a bit... Back on the concrete in the sun... Feel the energy off the crowd... Mile 4...

feeling good... Glad I have my cap on... It's starting to get hard... And harder to keep up this pace... If I slip back 15 seconds a mile that's ok.... Still going to get well under 6 hours... Keep taking the isotonic in... Seems to be working well... Mile 5... An ambulance ahead... Woh... Someone's collapsed... Probably dehydrated... Maybe they did not do the necessary training... Feel sorry for them... Thank god it's not me... I've done the training... I'll be ok... Mile 6... Getting harder but still running... Not going to run a 1hr 45 half marathon here... That would be stretching it a bit... Lets just keep up a good pace but not overdue it and save some in the tank for later... I know it's going to get harder... Half way through the run now... Great... Not long to go...

Then I can eat lots of food after I have finished and start my long awaited taper for Ironman Frankfurt in 3 weeks time... I am glad I am wearing this Ironman Frankfurt visor... Even though it's a finishers visor from last year wearing it in training and in this race is giving me extra strength... Thank god I need it... Anything to make me keep going... Feeling good... Mile 7... Getting harder and hotter... Lets get some salts... Grab some pretzels and lets try some red bull... A bit of caffeine... Mile 8... Do not think that red bull went down to well... Lets get a bit of water to and go back to the carbs... Its water of the head time... Need to cool my core down... Its great to do an official Ironman race in the UK finally...

Mile 9... Having to put a real effort in a couple of times a mile now to hit the target in my head... I know its not exactly even paced running and is giving me a worse time overall but it seems to be less painful running like this as most of the time I know I can push harder if I need to then slow down a bit when I have to get back on time for the mile... Revising my half marathon time in my head constantly... What was 15 seconds slower per mile is now 30 seconds slower per mile than my original plan but I am being smart... I am taking in the nutrition and cooling my body temperature at every aid station...

Mile 10... Not long to go now... A lot of people are walking... Not me... Some of them have 2 or 3 laps to go... Feel sorry for them... Not me... Of course some people have finished now... The top athletes... Just one lap to go for me... It is starting to hurt... Let's not overdue but lets push to the end...Pushing 90% effort just to keep running... It's taking a lot to keep going... Hang on a minute there is a young woman over taking me... Not having that... Lets put a bit of a spurt on... That's it... Back in front... Uh oh... She is coming up again... She must be good for her age group... Lets stay focused and go at the pace I want to go at... Run my own race... Better let her go past... She is running quicker than I want to... Fair play... Where do a;; these good athletes come from... I wonder... I guess there are a lot of people in the world...

Mile 11. The pain is nearly over... Keep running... Come on... I've ran this far in training several times this year... And I do run reps much quicker every week... Lets keep going 12 miles in... Lets push it now... Its taking 95% effort to keep running... Do not want to go flat out as do not want to pull a hamstring or get injured anywhere else... Also it's too painful... Also remember what Rachel Joyce said... Hold back a bit in the half marathon or will burn out for Frankfurt... Then Nick said you have to push harder after each mile... He's right.... It gets harder every mile... Just to stay at the same pace or even get near the pace I was running at when I started out... It gets harder.... Just half a mile to go... No one is going to overtake me now... Unless they are a super fast finisher...

I can hear the finish line... Awesome.... Look at the finish... No one near me... I can jog in... Look at the time... Well under 6 hours... Awesome... Lets jog slowly and enjoy the finish... Arms raised... High fives with some of the crowd... Awesome...

As I pass the finish line I have a great feeling... Loud music... Great atmosphere from the crowd for the athletes... Someone puts a medal round my neck... My legs ache... I am hot... And happy to stop.... Right lets keep walking so I do not seize up...

My mind turns to Frankfurt straight away. I make sure I keep walking on and off for the next 15 minutes whilst going in the athletes tent and taking advantage of the free food. The best food I remember is a giant pork burger... Nice... Just one each though... I could have eaten four of them... Some crisps for salts... Coconut water I think... Whatever it is I keep walking round.. stop for a minute and then walk round for a bit... Half an hour later I go back out and watch people come through the finish line... Then I go back to transition give my bike back to the Nirvana Team to take away for me.. Go to the shop to buy a Ironman UK 70.3 cap and some t-shirts for the family and watch people coming over the finish line. Its 7 hours since the start of the race... The look on people's faces finishing is priceless... Exultation, joy... For some of them you can tell it's overwhelming... The area after the finish line once you have been given the medal and before the exit into the athletes tent and the rest of the public area is the most revealing... There are people leaning against the railings... One or two of them are crying... You can tell it was a real journey for them. Maybe it was harder than they thought... Some of them exhausted... Some of them pumped up with excitement... Everyone has their own story for wanting to push themselves through so much pain... The story is even greater for the full Ironman races as the pain of completing a Half Ironman with a Full Ironman is so much more but as Half Ironman's Go Wimblewall has to be one of the hardest.

It was sunny all day from 10am as well which made it even harder.

I was really pumped up afterwards. My position had exceeded my expectations and that of my coach. I came 284th out of 1635 athletes. The swim took me 37 minutes, the bike 3hr 17 minutes and the run 1hr 52 minutes. It took me 5 hrs 55 minutes and 37 seconds including the transitions.

It was also the last days training off a hard week as well. In fact it was my final hard weeks training before I began my taper. Just three weeks to go until Frankfurt.

Ironman Frankfurt July 2014

Now its time for Ironman Frankfurt. I'd been preparing for this moment all season. Now I had 2 years of training in swim, bike and run behind me. What could I achieve? I had 2 targets – less than 10 hours a kind of dream goal and then less than 11 hours – a more realistic goal.

After Wimblewall my confidence was high. I'd had a really good performance, felt strong and the day after was the first day after my 3 week taper. I felt fantastic. As the days went buy I felt more rested and started to feel stronger. The sessions I did gave me even more confidence. I felt strong in the run reps, was going faster than ever in the swimming pool and my cycling felt good.

The week before Frankfurt I was starting to get excited and terrified at the same time. You know how it is when you work so hard for something but you have yet to achieve it. I wanted to do myself justice this time and get a new personal best time.

I had lost a bit of weight and got down to 80 kilos 3 weeks before the race. My usual weight was around 84 kilos. This was on Dave Scott's advice. It contradicted what Nick had said. Nick said be careful losing weight so soon before the race as I would lose my power. Looking back I was really spending too much energy thinking about the race throughout the whole year.

I was due to fly out on the Wednesday with race day being Sunday. I just started packing on the Tuesday afternoon and around 4.30pm I got my passport out.... Oh my god... It had expired... I punched the glass stairway in my house. Thank god it did not break but it really hurt my hand and it would hurt on and off for several weeks. I phoned the British passport office. Luckily they could get me an appointment for early the next morning but then I would have to wait for 3 hours to get my passport so I would miss my flight. I phoned Nirvana Europe and they were really helpful. They booked me on another flight later in the afternoon. I had to pay for another flight but I was still going to get there on the same day but in the evening instead of in the morning. It meant I was travelling on my own instead of with the other athletes, but I had to accept it. Jonathan from Nirvana, a really nice guy was still going to pick me up from the airport and drive me back to the hotel and my bike was being driven over so I was glad to have Nirvana to take some of the stress off me.

I decided to book myself into a hotel in the morning after the meeting and got a couple of hours sleep in between applying for my passport and receiving it. Frankfurt here we come. I was about to enter the Ironman European Championships. Yes! It was really going to happen... I felt strong... I took some sleeping tablets with me that I had got from the doctor... I usually used herbal sleeping tablets every now and then... I might use them everyday for a week or two and then not use them for months... I had some stronger ones from the doctor just in case.

I arrived at the main hotel where the pros were staying. The Grand Continental . It was awesome. Mega expensive at £250 a night but I really wanted to see the pros before and after the event. That made the whole experience more real and more motivating for me. I'd enjoyed seeing the pros before Ironman Austria the year before and got the same buzz out of it this time around. I had a good nights sleep the first night with the strong sleeping tablets that I had been given by my doctor and I really needed it.

I had gone out for a little run and walk to stretch my

legs after the flight.

The next morning I went out for a little run before breakfast as instructed by Nick my coach. Every session had been tailored for me and Nick had explained to me why I was doing each session as well, which was important.

I go down for breakfast and I walk straight past Frederick Van Lierde. No way the current Ironman World Champion was staying in the same hotel. Then a few moments later Sebastian Kienle walks past smiling – two time Ironman 70.3 world champion and as I write this Kona 2014 World Champion. I talk to Sebastian and he is very nice and he points out Jan Frodeno the 2008 Olympic World Champion to me… Jan is about to do his first full distance Ironman. He's a really nice guy.

There are a lot of athletes in the hotel. All of them look super fit. As I go in and out of hotel and walk around it there are a mixture of athletes, their supporters, Ironman staff and business people.

The food in the hotel was nice but mega expensive. It was €37 for the buffet at any time of the day. I would have used it every day but then I saw Frederick Van Lierde having burger and chips from the menu. I thought that I could save over €20 and eat the same pre race food as the current World Champion.

I decided to sit in on the pros media launch. It was advertised in the hotel. It was great to see all the pro's there and I managed to sit in on them giving one to one interviews with Ironman. Nobody asked me who I was. It was mainly pros and a few Ironman staff, photographers and a few journalists there.

I heard quite a touching interview with the reigning Ironman European Women's Champion Michelle Vesterby who spoke of how she was recovering from a crash only a few months before. At one time it looked like she would never be able to compete as a professional athlete again but just a few months later she was defending her title. She showed amazing strength and sensitivity in her interview... It was some guy from Ironman interviewing her on his mobile and I was sat less than six feet away. Just the three of us... I felt blessed being there... I congratulated her on her bravery... Next up was an interview with Jodie Swallow... She was one of the favorites of the race and came across as very motivated and charismatic. I had a chat with her afterwards and she was very friendly and wished her the best of luck for the race... I said I would like to interview her and she said she would email me before the race...

Looking back this became a distraction for me as I had told myself not to look at my email the days before the race but now I was going in every few minutes to see if Jodie had emailed me... I went out for a couple of bike rides the days before the race and found that I was going desperately slow as there were traffic lights everywhere. I was very worried about getting a puncture so did not ride very far. I ended up riding on the cycling track which goes across the run route of the race where I could go a bit quicker and made do with that.

However there was broken beer bottles in a few places, which made me even more anxious about getting a puncture. I rode a lot less than Nick had advised in the days before the race... I'd done the same thing in Austria as I had been worried about getting a puncture but was confident in my riding ability and just glad that I did not get a puncture...

I attended the pro race briefing again. Awesome. I had got Frederick Van Lierde to sign my race visor the day before to wish me luck. He was a very nice guy and struck me as being extremely focused on the race whilst being very approachable. I congratulate him for that as I imagine it's not easy to get the balance right. He was with his two children the day before and was driving around in an Ironman World Champion Van with his team. I asked him what it was like to be the fittest man in the world and asked his children what it was like to have a dad that was the fittest man in the world. He was very humble. I asked him how he got there and he said "by setting goals and working hard every day". Just goes to show that there are no secrets and no short cuts to success. At the pros briefing I was one of the last to arrive and just walked in. Everyone was sat in chairs apart from Frederick sat on the floor at the back in almost a yoga position and one of the women pros in another stretching position. I sat in between them doing similar stretches. Frederick smiled and said hello.

After the briefing I noticed none other than multiple world champion Natascha Badmann. She was full of smiles. She was having a blood test. I said I wanted to interview her and she said that's fine so I gave her my email address. She was not in the same hotel but said that we could meet up after the race. How cool was that? Pretty cool, I thought.

In the days before the race my sleep was pretty appalling. I used the strong sleeping tablets for 3 nights. The last night I used them they hardly worked... I was working really hard coming up for ideas for my new triathlon website 141triathlon.com and kept texting Daniel Hawksworth about it who I had been having conversations with. He was a super nice guy and of course Ironman UK champion. He was having a good season as well with quite a few podium places in full Ironman's and had come in the top 20 in the Ironman 2013 World Championships despite having a penalty on the bike. I emailed Harry Wiltshire my swim coach and he told me to "relax and enjoy it".

Race morning and I was up and ready. I had gone to the toilet probably 100 times in the night. I was not sure if I even slept at all... Setting myself up the transition the day before I had been very lucky... I'd got on a bus with my bike and lots of other athletes which was pretty crowded and I had got talking to a woman who had done a 100 mile race and 3 Ironman races... Then I walked off, said goodbye and 30 seconds later realized I had left all my transition gear in my rucksack on the bus! Oh my God, I gave my bike to a volunteer to look after and ran back to the bus, which was now full of other athletes leaving the transition area and stopped the bus, which was already moving. I said I had forgot my bag and luckily found it straight away. If I had left it another 10 seconds I may not have even be able to have enter the race or would have spent the whole day the day before trying to work out how to get all my gear in transition. In Frankfurt you give them your running gear and put it in a bag as Transition 1 and Transition 2 are in completely different areas so I was really lucky to have remembered my gear in time. Nick had told me to actually go to a quieter hotel and avoid all the hype and focus on my own race. He was 30 years into his Triathlon career and was a very consistent performer. I had managed to avoid the Expo for the main part, which can drain you without you realizing it. I got to transition and got al my gear sorted out. Then back to the hotel for a spaghetti bolognese and bed.

The night before my second Ironman I went to bed early around 8pm. I did not take a sleeping tablet this time in case they worked to well. It was the worst nights sleep that I had had ever. I kept getting up and going to the toilet... I had been hydrating with Dioralyte the previous 2 days and was almost certainly over doing it probably taking twice as many as Nick advised...

I had been taking vitamins and protein shakes throughout my training throughout the year and taper but did not take them with me to Frankfurt. I was taking so many things with me and I had already so much kit in my bag that I took over with my bike that I did not want to overdo the packing and be charged more money by Nirvana for packing too much gear. I was pretty confident that my taper, reduction in caffeine until race day and the creatine would give me a big enough boost come race day. I'd done the training so felt confident in my ability to deliver a good time.

Anyway, race morning. Up at 4.00am and down to breakfast straight away. A big bowl of porridge some scrambled eggs and a double coffee. Same as I had had for Wimblewall and that had worked out well. This time I had a bit more scrambled egg and a bit more porridge. Back in the room and I meticulously put on my P20 sun cream and got my race gear on. Tri shorts and tri top... Then it was downstairs to get ready for the race. Just outside the hotel there were frequent buses going to the race start. I got to there nice and early and got to the transition area. Time to put the drinks on my bike... then disaster struck! I put some of my drink in on my specialized shiv and I could not suck it out of the straw. Nick had put it in for me and tested it where it worked but then we had to re do it as it would be contaminated if we left it after testing it for race day. Oh my god! I could not find anyone else with the same bike that was there to help. I asked a volunteer to help and he said to try the mechanics. There were only two mechanics I could see for the 2800 athletes.

I rushed over and after queuing for a couple of minutes found a mechanic and told him the problem. He said he knew the bike and could fix it. I also asked if he could check the tyres and he said he would. He had just done one of the pros bikes and he said that he was a friend of Jan Raphael, a top German Pro and that Jan did not have a clue about the maintenance of his bike either even though he was a great athlete.

I told this mechanic that he had saved my life and he was such a nice guy as well. He managed to turn a massive panic attack into a celebration for me and I even had time to take a quick photo of the both of us together.

So my bike worked ok, and now it was time to get the wetsuit on. That always took longer than I thought it would... I remembered to use my rub for my neck and walked down to the start. I was one of the first age groupers to get in the water. My plan was to stay on the front line... Just 9 days before I had my best swim ever in the pool. A 4km swim non-stop in 1 hr. 22 minutes. Three weeks before I had my best competitive swim at 1.9km in 37 minutes...
This time there was an Australian exit, which was unlike Austria... As I got in position I realized that I was on the wrong side... I had gone too far left and we were swimming more to the right... It seemed like the more aggressive swimmers were all to the right so I moved up a bit and ended up in the middle of everyone. Harry had shown me some tricks how to swim over people, exactly how to start in the water so I was already in swimming position and it proved that I was going to need all his tricks here to help me...

The pros went off.... And the top age groupers... They

had started 15 minutes before... There was extreme adrenaline before the race... It's hard to explain... Flashes of massive excitement combined with absolute terror of the massive journey ahead. I had never been fitter in my life and never been so pumped up... Very similar feelings to the first Ironman except this time I knew I could finish it as I had already finished one. This time I was a better swimmer, biker and runner and a more experienced athlete.

The gun went off and it was game on. Pandemonium. The first minute there were arms and legs everywhere. I was swimming over the top of people. People were swimming over me... A couple of minutes in and I get a kick in the face... Uh oh... My goggles come off... I stop and put them back on and get people swimming all over me... Back in to my front crawl straight away... I cannot see anything out of either eye... I stop again after 5 or 6 seconds and then it gets even more congested... I maneouvre the goggles quickly and set off again... At least this time I can see out of one eye... I swim for another 5 minutes like this and as the race thins out a bit and more and more people start to overtake me I manage to stop go over on my back and readjust my goggles.. Bingo now I can see properly... Thank god for that... Now I get into a rhythm and start to focus on each stroke. Harry Wiltshire had told me that when put my right arm under the water to imagine it's a harpoon and do not finish the stroke to early... The to pull through all the way and recover quickly... I felt good but it was not going as well as I had hoped... I did not seem to be able to draft anybody as I had a few weeks before in Wimblewall... The swimmers were better on average here and I was not going at the same pace. At Wimblewall I had come up every 5 strokes and taken a look by pushing my right arm down further and taken a look without breaking the stroke. This led to my being able to sight easier. This time would do this only once a minute or so…

I was confident going round the buoys where Harry told me to swim on my bike and roll over back onto my front round the buoys and really accelerate out to avoid being trampled on… This worked beautifully at Wimblewall. In Frankfurt it worked ok. At one buoy I kept getting kicked in the head and actually stopped and shouted at the person doing it who took notice and carried on swimming. It was a woman. As I said it I could see a Marshall on a boat so thought I better shut up or I might get disqualified. Talk about wasting energy that was what I was doing…

As I got out at the Australian exit it was a little over half-way distance… I had calculated that I was 3 or 4 minutes slower than I had planned at halfway. Not a disaster but enough to really annoy me… I enjoyed the second half of the swim much more as it was less congested and I got into a rhythm… I also got a buzz out of doing it… the buzz from exercising kicked in and I knew my worst discipline was ending… I could also see the crowd cheering and it was a great atmosphere… I got to the swim finish and I was quite a bit quicker than in Austria… where I swam 1hr 34 minutes. This time I was 1hr 22 minutes. I had thought I would be going round in 1hr 15 to 1hr 20 max so was disappointed but happy to finish stage 1 of 3 although everyone knows that once you have finished the swim in the Ironman you are nowhere near one third of the race in distance, time or effort, just one third of the types of sports have finished…

It was going to be a long day. In Euphoric mode I picked up someone else's swim hat… Then I jogged up to transition, took a look back and was disappointed to see a lot less swimmers in the water than I had hoped. Still now for my strength the bike… Transition

1... I ran into the tent, ran straight past my bag and wasted 10 seconds looking for it... Then realized it was way too tight... I sat down and spent 30 seconds trying to open my bag. Impossible... I had knotted it too tight and into too many knots... I had to rip it open... This made me worry that I was going to lose my expensive wetsuit, hats and goggles when they moved all the transition bags to be nearer to the end of the race... I sat down and had my salt drink – 4 sachets of Dioralyte already mixed with water... Took off my wetsuit and put my socks on with wet feet and gave my bad to a volunteer saying there was a hole in it and too look after the wetsuit. He said "ok... I have it". So on the bike... Most of the bikes had already gone... There are 3 or 4 people getting on their bike at the start of the bike I run straight past them and pick up a few places and then as I cannot clip in "someone behind me shouts" as I am blocking several people...

Then it's off to the start of the bike... Nick and I had spoken on the phone a couple of times whilst I was in Frankfurt and we had been texting each other quite a lot as well. He had texted me to go in a certain gear on the bike... This is something that we later realized had got lost in translation... Let me explain... I had planned to ride the bike one or two gears off the hardest gear then in the text I thought Nick meant for me to ride 3-4 gears off the hardest gear... He meant that was just the gear that I should start in and then get up to the planned gear... In reality this meant that I was going easier on the first part of the course, which was flat... Anyway the Ironman is a really long day so this was a minor point considering everything else that was to go on...

In Ironman you are only allowed to ride on one side of the road... Also you are not allowed to draft... I could not believe how slow everyone was riding and how many people there were... I could overtake a group of people every now and then but at the start of the bike it seemed like there was a Marshall going past on his motorbike every 30 seconds... There were a couple of people really going for it on the bike but in order to do so you had to go on the other side of the road to overtake which should be a definite penalty if you were spotted and its also impossible to just ride in front of someone who is in a group of 50 riders all spaced out without someone being liable for a penalty... This meant that the start of the bike I was very cautious... worried about being penalized... frustrated when I felt I could have overtaken hundreds of people... Oh I wish I could have swam to my potential... It would have made the start of the bike easier and I would have been nearer some better bikers as well...

Anyway I got my nutrition in starting with my carbs drink and then chewing on my energy bar bit by bit... I had a clear nutrition plan that went totally out of the window for 2 reasons... At the first aid station I grabbed what I thought was a carb drink that turned out to be a bottle of coke... I was not planning on having any more caffeine until half way through the run as the more you use it during the day the less of an effect is meant to have... Perhaps a minor point but I let it lay with my head...

The next point was probably a bit more important... This time around I decided to pee on my bike for the first time ever... It saved me stopping for the loo. However it felt pretty disgusting doing it and when I did it I was worried about getting a penalty... However what I did not realise until the day after the race when I was doing a video about it was that I made a stupid mistake throughout the whole bike ride... I would pee in my pants and then sip my gels and put them in my shorts... What an idiot... All I realized as I was riding hard and it was getting hotter was that every time I got my gels out they had been washed away... This led to me having probably only around 40% of my gels... So I had not had enough carbs on the ride... I ended up taking in more drink and then an energy bar and a banana later on in the ride that was ok but it was possible the cause of nutrition/toilet problems later in the race which I will explain later...

The atmosphere in Frankfurt was fantastic. We got up the first hill where the cobbles were and the atmosphere was even better... It was dead easy compared to what I thought it would be... However what was really worrying me was that I was starting to feel tired after 30 miles on the bike and the bottom of my feet were hurting... where the cleats were... The bottom of my feet had never hurt on the bike before... I think this may be because I was not used to riding with wet socks...

As the bike went on the weather was getting hotter and hotter... My time was ok for the first 28 miles but then as the time went on I was getting more tired and what I had anticipated before of being a 5hr 20 – 5hr 30 minute bike ride turned into a grit for survival... Eventually I was pleased to get in at 5hr 58 minutes...

I was pleased to get it over and done with... the transition was great as you give your bike to a volunteer... I needed the loo and queued for one... Two people jumped in front of me and after standing there for 30 seconds I thought I just better carry on...

Before the race I had planned on doing a 3hr 50 marathon... By the time I was finishing the bike I thought that this was going to be impossible... After 80 miles on the bike I had felt really ill... I took a power bar that saved me and by the time I got to the start of the run I was worried.

However when I actually started running I felt great... I was disappointed with my swim and bike time and was 40-50 minutes slower than I thought I was going to be at that stage... I remember when I got to the start of the run the year before in Austria and my legs had felt like wood... This time they felt really flexible... I ran out of transition and had to consciously slow down a few gears after 30 seconds, then a minute and 3 minutes as I was running above my planned pace... My plan was to run each 10km in 55 minutes and then spurt at the end.

One thing I was not expecting was how hot I was... Especially my head... I did not have an aero helmet on the bike and had being cooling my body down a lot on the bike so could not understand it... I just assumed it was because I was not used to training or racing in the heat.

A few Kilometres in and I was running exactly to pace... Just feeling hot... Especially my head... I needed the loo and had flatulence but was running so well that I did not want to stop and lose momentum... I was taking carb drinks at the aid stations... (no gels, which I think, turned out to be a mistake)... I'd had a mini box of Pringles in Transition 2, which meant I had my salts... I'd just shoved them in my mouth all at once and they tasted great with the salt just as Nick had said they would.

So through 10km in 55 minutes... I was spot on for the perfect run... Then things started to go wrong.... I just felt hotter and hotter... Similar to feeling faint but it was not faint... I could not understand it... Then uh oh... I needed the toilet... big time.... And I do not mean a wee! I could see two cubicles on the other side of the road... I had to go round a corner and it was on the opposite side... I thought about going straight to the cubicle but thought I could get disqualified... I had to stop running or I was going to have an accident... Then I realized I had to walk quickly... I was 30 metres from the cubicles, when I had a choice.... Either pull my shorts down and pooh a massive diaorrhea (sorry there is no other way to describe it) in front of 200 people and maybe get disqualified or take it like a man or a toddler (however you want to perceive it) and then go and clean myself up in cubicle.... Thank god I got in the cubicle.

Lets just say.... 9 minutes later I came out of the toilet as quick as I could... There had been several knocking in between from probably similarly desperate athletes but this was no time for charity. Coming out I was nearly a broken man... I was pleased I was clean but devastated that my run time was spoilt... Also I was finding it harder to run as well... I set off and never regained the previous pace I had been running at.

The atmosphere was great... I still aimed to run from aid station to aid station... There was an aid station every 2 kilometres... but I was starting to walk longer after each of them... and then another athlete told me that my neck was bright red and that I should go to medical... Eureka! Ah that was it! That was why I was feeling so light headed. I must have been sunstroke.
I turned my visor the other way round... Every time I got to the aid station I was now running with ice in my hands and even asking the volunteers to spray my neck with water... When I found medical someone put some sun cream on so I was careful not to wet my neck after that but the damage was already done to my time.

What seemed like a million times I wanted to give up

but I knew I would regret it if I did... I knew in my head that I could still run under 5 hours if picked it up towards then end and I knew I would still get a personal best time... but gone was the plan of going in under 11 hours and cuckoo seemed the dream of going under 10 hours in an Ironman this day of any day... Qualifying for Kona was at best a delirious fantasy for someone of my ability or my ability to execute my imaginary talent.

Kilometres 11-31 were some of the darkest hours of my life. However with 10km to go as hard as it was I could see a light... By this time some of the food and drink that I had been experimenting with as my nutrition plan had gone out of the window was kicking in and healing my body, it was getting later in the afternoon so it was cooling down and soon I knew I would have completed my second Ironman... All these thoughts seemed to give me a spur... Also of the people left I had more arms bands on than most of them had on which meant I was a lap or two ahead and most of them were walking or going slower.

For the final 10km I picked myself up and shuffled along... I managed to jog the whole way and walk the aid stations but not walk in between much at all. During the last 10km I only remember a couple of people over taking me.

So just 1km to go... When you get near the end you get the euphoric feeling... All that training... all the sacrifices... all the pain of the day... worthwhile.... In my head I was thinking I can get near 12 hrs 30 minutes if I keep going.

Then the sight of the finish... A long finishing chute... possibly the longest in any of the Ironman's and red carpet... nice and soft.

It feels fantastic to get there. I want to finish strong. I start high fiving people every few metres. I jog as quick as I can without falling over. I see someone ahead of me and there is nobody behind. I manage to overtake the only person that had over taken me over the previous 5km. Admittedly he had stopped to run across the finishing line with his children which kind of got in the way of my finish but that was one more place gained.

I had survived and finished. The toughest day of the year had ended. I had dreaded it and longed for it all year and despite being way outside the time that I was aiming for I was extremely proud of having completed my second Ironman. At the finish line there were some volunteers giving a giant medal out which was nice. I had it round my neck and grabbed some of the nutrition on display. I walked on a few metres and saw a few giant ice buckets with other people stood in them. That looked nice I thought so I got in one. The iced water went all the way up to my waist. I stayed in it for 3 or 4 minutes and then decided to go into the finisher's tent and get some serious food in. I had one giant pork role. The food on offer was not as good as Ironman Austria. There you could have helped yourself to whatever you wanted. Here you were limited to one giant roll although there was lots of other food to munch on and lots of drinks as well. Considering all the effort everyone had put in to make the start line and get to the finish I think they got this wrong and should be more generous.

I was conscious of getting my nutrition in and just glad that I was still alive and healthy. I was walking around a fair bit trying not to get too stiff but would sit down every now and then to eat and then get back up.

On my mind straight away was that I felt better physically and mentally than I did after finishing my first Ironman so that was a good sign. Deep inside I was disappointed with my time and performance but proud that I stuck at it and kept going. In my head I was questioning what went wrong and then thinking that I had the perfect years training and perfect warm up 70.3 but did not execute the race as planned. Big disappointment and delight for finishing. It was a strange sensation.

After half an hour eating, drinking, walking, sitting down and brief conversations with people I watched a few people crossing the finishing line and decided to go back and get my bike from transition.

I had to get my non race clothes on to warm up as it was now getting cold and then go back to transition which seemed like miles away. I was so tired that I gave a volunteer my kit bag and she very kindly looked after it for me until I returned 10 minutes later with my bike. I was riding my bike back through the crowded transition area and behind the finish line and nearly fell off a few times as I kept stopping. Every now and then I would shout "come on" to the exhausted people who still had a few miles left to run, jog or crawl over the line.

My initial plan was to ride back to the hotel that was a 10-minute spin away under normal circumstances. By the time I got back to the finish line which was on the way back to the hotel I was so hungry again that I gave my bike to a couple of volunteers to look after and started munching and sitting down for another 20 minutes. I was absolutely famished.

Then I got back to the hotel through the expo centre.

The rest of the evening is a bit of a haze. I showered, ate downstairs and had a deep sleep. I had a text from Nick congratulation me on a new personal best time. I spoke to my partner and children, answered a few texts and went back to sleep.

The next day I had my giant breakfast. I could see Sebastian Kienle grinning round the hotel. He was the new European champion. I went to the awards ceremony and had a good chat with Jodie Swallow who had been leading the women's race the whole way until she blew up somewhat on the run.

The awards ceremony was miles from the hotel which was a bit testing. I got a taxi there ok and managed to blag a lift back with one of the Ironman vehicles taking the pros back to the hotel.

I also managed to find an Ironman member of staff who gave me two event swim hats. My swim hat and goggles disappeared between handing them to a volunteer during the race and then collecting them after the race. No doubt due to the massive hole I had torn in the bag during my clumsy transition. Thank god my wetsuit was still there.

I stayed over one more day and night after the race to recharge a bit and then just wanted to get back home.

My coach Nick picked me up at the airport the next afternoon and we chatted all the way back. It was great to see him and he was very encouraging. We talked about the race. The good things I did and the things that I could do better next time. I told him of hurting my hand the week before the race, selecting the wrong gears on the bike, the insomnia the nights before the race, grabbing the coke bottle early on in the run, nutrition, how hot I felt, getting the nutrition and peeing wrong on the bike.

Nick said that the most likely thing that contributed to the sub par performance was probably missing the flight, the stress that came with that and the lack of sleep days before the race. He said nine out of 10 times I would have got the time I wanted around 11.00 hours and not 12 hrs 31 minutes.

My final splits and positions were. 1723 overall out of 3205 athletes. I was bitterly disappointed with the position as I had wanted to be between the top 400 and the top half. My total time was 12:31:39 . I was upset I had not gone under 11 hours or even under 12 hours but please with a new personal best time beating the 13 hours 17 minutes I had taken in Austria the year before, My swim time was 1 hr 22 minutes, my bike time was 5 hrs 58 minutes (I had expected to go 5 hrs 30 minutes) and my run fell apart at 4 hours 59 minutes where I had hoped to go 3 hours 50 minutes or at least 4 hours ish.

I guess they do not call it the hardest one day endurance event in the world for nothing.

We decided that I was going to do another Ironman the following year. I was so happy to see my kids and proud to wear my new Ironman Frankfurt finishers T-Shirt. I was still delighted to have completed my second Ironman but felt that I had trained well the whole year, nailed the 70.3 race in Wimblewall and not executed the big race in Frankfurt properly.

I really wanted some time off from the day to day training and pressure of setting a massive and wanted to stop thinking about Ironman for a while. Of course everyone I saw was asking me about it and it was good to tell them. Soon enough I would be on holiday with my family... In fact 3 weeks later I was in Crete on an all you can eat holiday with my partner and two wonderful children. There would be no running and biking for me then although I must admit I was swimming every day.

I knew I was planning to do an Ironman the following year... After all I would be one year older... One year more experienced and had not done myself justice in the long distance race... Whether I had the dedication, focus and life balance to do another one you'll have to wait and see...

It was becoming clear however that qualifying for Kona on merit was years away for me and probably way out of my potential especially considering I had other things in my life that I viewed as equally important and more important than Ironman. I thought of an interview with American pro Andy Potts. He seems a really genuine guy. He said that there "is this obsession in Ironman which has you going for a fast time and a top position. He said that how well you do in an Ironman does not determine how good you are as a person". This struck quite a frisson with me when I heard it... I had started Ironman to get fitter and to be part of something bigger than myself... It still inspired me but did not want it taking over my life...

I knew that next time around I would be less obsessed with it... and spend less time over thinking it... I had hear other people say this time and time again to calm down and not over think it but it did not really register until I started training again for my next Ironman although by August 2014 I did not know which Ironman that would be...

I hope you have found some useful information, fun and inspiration in this second memoir...

In the mean time... Happy dreaming... Happy goal setting and happy racing.. As 2013 Ironman World Champion Frederick Van Lierde said when I interviewed him to be successful – work hard and set goals... Its not rocket science.. Just commons sense and "dedication" as 16 times world darts champion Phil Taylor told me...

Notes and Training Leading up To 2nd Ironman Frankfurt 2014 and the week after.

Early December 2013 long run:
2 hour run 13.39 miles c palace park all 150-160 heart rate.

Dec 11 run reps below 180 2 x 2 6m 45, 7m 10, 7m 7, 7m 3. (Slower than before – shows how hard it is and how you have to pace yourself. Consistency is the key).

Dec 2nd 1.9km swim time 42 mins

(Nov 28th - 38.19 - 1800 metre if add up 2 x 900 metre reps with gap... After few days ill)

29 Dec 40 min run 5.49 miles
30th Dec 60min run 7.39 miles
31st Dec 2hr run 13.12 mile
1 st jan 1hr 40m 11.1 miles (no nutrition tired, slight ankle ache)
2nd jan - no training. Ankle swollen. Nothing major but best to be safe.
3rd jan - 60min run 7.39 miles
4th jan - off (resting ankle).
5th jan off

Week starting 20th jan 2014....
Hi nick,
Did all sessions this week.
Mon 90min bike - 25.4 miles. 18.6 av speed. Difficulty 15/20. Water only during.
Tue did swim - straight into 100s. No warm up. Did 11x100s. 1m 45, 1m 53, 2m, 2m 1, 2m 5 x 5, 2m 8, 2m 12. Did warm down 2 x 100 float on front (not sure how to do drill on back). Did warm down front and backstroke.

Bike 60m 180watts off and 230 watts max on. 18mph average inc warm up and down. 15/20 difficulty as 30 minutes after swim.

Wed run reps 3 x1 mile. 6m 13, 6m 13, 6m 10. Good talking to Jim.

Thursday - did brick session as guided. Felt strong even with a heavy cold.

Friday - did most of swim session. Tired with cold.

Did 500 meters warm up ok.

Did pyramid wrong way round.

2 x 300m 6m 31, 6m 41... 3 x 200m 4m 29, 4m 35, 4m 36, 1 x 400m 9m 24. Did 200 metre warm down breast stroke and back stroke. Felt good to do longer swim as I've neglected it a bit the last month. Need to be more consistent. Overall did all the sessions. Knackered now and look forward to break tomorrow.

Harry said swim 100s, 4000metres.

Thanks. On the 11th lets just do the swim lesson, video and follow up

5k best 20m 53
10k best 46m 40
Half marathon best 1hr 51
21 mile best 3hrs 15
Marathon - during ironman

Week 27th jan:

Sunday turbo 120 mins 32.7 miles

Mon turni 110 mins 30.6 miles. 146 heart rate at end of 2 of 4 210-240 bpm.

Tue big swim - did full 25min warm up. Thought Did all 22 x 50 metres but only 18 on watch? :). (Maybe wishful psychology ha). All between 54 seconds and 1m 1 seconds. Only 2 above minute and that was when people got in the way. :) Did 15-20 breaths between lengths. Did full 400 metre kick with float

warm down.
Bike 180off 220-230w on
16 miles all +1. Did bike 9pm at night so took it a bit easier. 150-160 warm up and warm down.
Wed: run reps with gym. 4 x 2 miles. 7m 4 sec, 7m 5sec, 7m 8sec, 7m 8sec, 7m 8sec, 7m 7sec, 7m 7s, 6m 48 seconds. Jim said to sprint the last 300 metres so i did. My heart rate was below 185 the whole time. Mostly between 170-180. Sometimes on second laps it was 181-183 for the last 200 metres of the mile. Felt strong and quicker.
Thu swim: 4 x 400s - 8m 25s 8m 45s 9m 10s 9m 35s

Norlond combine 50tt race 10/5-16/5. Sub 1hr 4 addiscomber sub 2hr 10 norlond. Sub 4hr 35 in hounslow and district wheelers 100tt.

regular. When I get back perhaps I can work with you on it if you can spare one Thursday evening I can perhaps analyse and video you at Trinity school pool where Blackheath Harriers train 20.30-21.30hrs.

Week 2nd feb
Sunday 11.5 mile run 1hr 45m
Monday - did session
Tue- Swim - did reps and
Did turbo at night finished at 11.15pm. Water only except a rice cake half way through. :) knackered.

March 5th

Nick said today I should be running half marathon at 7m 30 pace - 1hr 37 mins and soon should be able to do a half marathon in 1hr 25 min.

Nick said ballbuster 2015 time should 3hrs 10 - 3hrs 15. I want to go under 3hrs... 3hr 5 mins would get me third in 40-49 age group..

Mid range running not for long runs
300-350 grams

Do I get another pair of Asics men's gel Oberon 6 trainer..

Mon March 15th
Run 33 min 3.33 miles
Turbo 60 16.4 miles

Tue March 16th
Turbo 90 25.2 miles - held power ok. Did b4 swim. Swim warm
Up was quicker than reps. 600metre warm up in under 12 minutes. Swim reps 1500 x 100s took 32 minutes total - between 59 seconds and 1 minute 10. Did 1hr 30 mins after turbo so tired from that.

Wed march 17th
Run reps 6 x 1km all between 3m 42 and 3m 45 secs. Had less to eat before hand and stomach hurt less. Took 15-20 breaths at end of each rep then straight into jogging. It was quite hot so really pleased with result.

Fri 19th march
Rest day

Sat 20th March

Did all the swim reps. Fastest was 3m 30 slowest was 4m 26 at end. Ised pull buoy and paddles for 9 of the 10 reps. All together for 2000m it took 41 mins 30 seconds. (30 seconds rest in between).

1hr break and then x 10 hill reps.

First 4m 30, last was 3m 26.. Average was just about 4 minutes. Gradually getting quicker. Could not really get heart rate above 160 though.

Sunday 21st march
1hr 10min ride 20 miles. Up to Biggin Hill + back. Came back early. Dressed to cold. It was horrible. Exhausted need a rest and mental break.

Sat 22nd march
Turbo 2hrs 20m. 39.5 miles. Av sp 17.5.

Mon 24th march
Did turbo 18.3 miles. Av sp 17.8.

Tuesday 25th march.
Swim
warm up - swam with 1 arm for 10 lengths and rest chicken wing. Breathing reps 500 metres 10mins 8 secs. Main reps 10 x 100s in 20 mins 48 seconds total. 59 secs to 1 m 6 per 50 metres slowest.

Turbo
Did turbo. Held power fine. 16.7 miles. Just had half bottle of water. No fan in garage as dangerous with kids.

Wed 26th march
Did all run reps with Jim.. X 5 1ks 3m 52 - 3m 55. Felt ok. It was windy, cold and freezing

Thu 27th march
Swim 4km time trial.. 1hr 31 minutes. 1km at 21 mins. 1500 m at 33m. 1900m at 42mins. 3000m at 68m.

Fri 28th march
Rest day... Great news spoke to nick on phone.... My 4km swim time was 1 hr 31 mins in pool. Through 3km

in 68 mins... Nick says that my ironman split will be around 70mins for the swim adding wetsuit and race conditional... Awesome... That's 24 minutes quicker than Klagenfurt 2013.

Sunday 30th march
2hr run- battery went dead. 5 laps of Crystal Palace park. Sip of water and water on head at 40mins and 1hr 20mins. Got quite hot. About 12 1/2 miles estimate.

Monday 31st march
Did turbo session. 18.4mph plus1.

Tuesday 1st april
Did turbo first 29.5 miles. 1hr 45mins. (Did not do the last 10 minutes at 190watts - had to fit work in).

Did swim 2 hours after turbo... Held times ok 15-25 seconds breaks. 1200m 11m 39seconds. Started at 1.49 per 100m pace ended at 2.00m per 100. On warm down did 200m float kicks and 200 metre fist drills. (Feel like I am getting into a nice rhythm with arms and using my back muscles more).

Wednesday 2nd april
6 x 1km reps between 3m 40
And 3m 50secs. 3m 49, 48, 45, 44, 42...

Thursday 3rd april
Did 2hr hilly turbo. Held power. Felt hard. Got a cold and not much sleep.

Friday 4th april.
Really bad cold. almost did
Not do it but amazing what 2 coffees can do. Swim reps... 400warm up - fists and one arm. 500m breathing drills. 4 x 500s with paddles and pull buoy.

Cold worse today. Did this mornings swim session ok though. Full warm up and warm down. 400s were at 8m 13, 8m 25, 8m 35, 8m 44, 8m 58. Used paddles and pull buoy. Going to skip todays turbo and rest for Sunday mornings big 20 mile run. Knackered. :)

Saturday 5th april
Day off. Bad cold... In bed.. Stayed in... Kids in garden...

Sunday 6 th april
Big run... Dulwich park... Meant to be 20 miles or 25 miles if do not feel good. Aim for 7m 30 pace... Held it at start but not at end... 15 miles in 1hr 55 mins... Raining at start but felt better by end as it was over. :)

Monday 7th april
40m spin and 10 minute run... Legs feel fine...

Tuesday 8th april
Swim 12 x 100m reps 24 mins
75min bike.... 22.3 miles all plus 1 gradient... Av speed 18.2....

Wed 9th april
Run warm up...strides... 5 x 1km
Reps all at 3m 45s. Did not do 6 th
One. Warm down...

Thu 10th april
Swim reps.. Wu.. 6 x 200
Paddles and pull buoy. Did 7 by mistake. Lost count. Here are times.
3m 38, 3m 57, 3m 54, 3m 59, 4m 01, 4m 09, 4m 12, 4m 03,
Hill reps on bike straight after (30 minutes by time i drove home and got changed. Had energy bar and protein bar straight after swim and took high 5 energy

drink on bike.

Hill rep times, 4m 29, 4m 12, 4 m 04, 3m 49, 3m 45, 3m 36, 3m 39, 3m 30, 3m 22, 3m 03.

Really went for it on the last one my legs were shaking when i stopped.

Feel great. Cold very nearly gone.

Looking forward to next weeks easy week.

Friday 11th april
Brick session.
65 mins turbo hill reps.. Held power just about up to 350 watts then 27 minute run at 3.41 miles

Sat 12th april off

Sun 13th april
2hrs turbo pyramid. 10mins each at150w, 160, 170, 180, 190, 200, 190, 180, 170, 220, 165,155

Monday 14th april
A rest day on a Monday wow...

Tuesday 15th april
Swim reps 1100 metres - 22 mins 9 seconds. Did warm up quite quickly with less breaks. Only had the 15 or 30 second breaks as instructed for the reps. All the 50 metre reps were under 1 minute - 56 seconds to 1m. The 100 reps were just over 1 minute laps.

Turbo - did the lactate threshold in the evening. Held power just about.

Wednesday 16th april
5 run reps x1 km. 3mins 48 secs each.

Thursday 17th april
65 mins sweetspot

Friday 18th april
Break Easter in Gloucester

Saturday 19th april
Day off training as in Gloucester for Easter. First time 2 days off training in a row since October 2013 or maybe Christmas 2013.

Sunday 20th april
First time out on time trial bike. Wow. Took 15 minutes to get used to the gears then the rest of the 2hrs was spent getting used to the speed, steering, gears and wind... Up to biggin hill and westerham and back. 34 miles in just under 2 hours. Top speed 38.4 mph... Pleased that got back up biggin hill 10% climb with relative ease... Did get moved in the wind a bit...

Monday 21st april..
Nick weekly call since being in Majorca start of march...
90 minute spin... 230 watts at 105 rpm webt down a gear... 28 miles...

Tuesday 22nd april
Did the swim 8.30 this morning. 29mins 10 secs for 14 x 100m reps. Between 56 seconds and 1 m 6sec 50metre laps. Full warm up as warm down and no more than 30 second breaks for reps.

Bike - 90m turbo. 27.3 all plus 1.

Wednesday 23rd april
6 x 1km run reps. 3m 30-3m 40
3m 32, 3m 40, 3m 40, 3m 44, 3m 41, 3m 43. Did not feel too good before i started but felt better as i went on.

Thursday 24th April
Bike 120 sweetspot. 4 x 20 mins at 230 watts.. Cut last 20mins into 10mins. It hurt. 31.3 miles....

Friday 25th of April.
900metre swim warm up. (200 fists and 200 one arm, 500 breathing drills), 4 x 400m with paddles and pull buoy - times 7m 22, 7m 42, 8m 2 seconds, 8m 18 seconds. Drove home and running within 25 minutes. Just a glass of water. Ran 10.25 miles in 90 minutes around c palace park. Had one gel at 60 minutes. Home - protein drink, five alive drink and banana straight away...

Saturday 26th of April

Sunday 27th of April
Bike - 26.34 miles in 1hr 9m 19sec
Av sp 22.8. Got lost on the time trial after 1 minute - turned left off the a road and into a country lane. Started going up a hill and realised i got it wrong so had to stop and turn around. Otherwise would have got an estimated 1hr 4 minute time. I asked them to dnf as i lost another 5 minutes for missing my start line. Felt good on the bike though - no drink just a gel at 30 minutes. and run felt even better.
Glass of water when getting changed and
Ran 3.77 miles in 30mins

Monday 28th of April
60 minute aerobic run 6.85 miles in 60 minutes. Felt good. Quite hot.

Tuesday 29th April
Swim - 900metre warm up. 30 x 50s reps - started off 1m 52 pace, held this for first 800metres, then went down to 1m 53 pace until 1100metres, 1m 54 pace at 1300 metres and 1m 55 pace by the end. 28mins 55

seconds for 1500 metres. Pleased with that.

Did not do today. Doing tomorrow instead.

Wednesday 30th April
70minute turbo - held power ok
Should have done yesterday but could not fit it in

Run reps 2hrs after turbo
6 x 1km reps, 3m 30, 3m 31, 3m 45, (stopped for the loo) 3m 55, 3m 53, 3m 45

Thursday 1st may
900m swim warm up. 500 breathing drills, 400 one arm.
10 x 200s. Started at 1m 49pace - ended at 1m 53m pace. 2000 metres in 28 minutes. 500m kick warm down.

Friday 2nd
Turbo 60 minutes but worked out as 40 minutes. Did i do it right. Hard but Easier than i thought.

Saturday off

Sunday 4th may
Time trial 25tt 1hr 5 mins. 5.6 mile run in 46mins.

Monday 5th may
40min run 5 miles.
Spoke to Dave scott on the phone. He said to lose weight - get even weight 3 weeks b4 race. First time i spoke to him was august 2013.

Tuesday 6th may
Pool closed til 1pm so did 70m turbo first. Held power

and cadence fine. Did swim an hour later. Full warm up and warm down. Started at 1m 52 pace went to 1m 53m
Pace at 500m.

Wednesday 7th may
4 x 1km run reps. Fastest four ever. Last time went above 3m 40
After 2 reps. This time. 3m 33, 3m 33, 3m 38, 3m 38.

Thursday 8th may
3km swim time trial 65mins 38 seconds.

Friday 9th may
Bike neuro muscular endurance. Held power. Feel strong. Massage and taped lower back.

Looking at how hilly the rides i have done and are going to do today. Interesting stats.
Austria 7829 feet climbing
Germany 5281 feet climbing
Hell of ashdown 104km
6400 feet 2000m climbing
Wimblewall 5905 feet climbing

Nick weekly coaching call advice.
Work on hip flexors, buttocks and lower back with roller... Forget about weight and strength training too much. Yoga poses good.

Saturday 10th may day off

Sunday 11th may
50mile tt 2hrs 15m followed by 3.6 mile run in 28 mins.

Monday 12th may
Swim 900m warm up. 15 x 100m in 30m 27seconds

Tuesday 13th of may
Did 2/3 of turbo session as spent day with my daughter Anna and watched time trial champion michael Hutchinson give a talk

Wednesday 14th of may
Run reps. Warm up 1 lap. 5 x 1 mile reps. 6m 08s, 6m 10, 6m 22, 6m 20, 6m 18. 2 laps warm down.

Thursday 15th may
900m warm up. 400 with one arm and fists. 500 breathe drills. 4 x 400s with paddles and pull buoy 7m 12, 7m 20, 7m 40, 7m 49.

Skin suit saves 30watts per 430 watts
Lower head position 30 watts per 430w
1 kilo lighter only 5 watts
Visor on helmet 2 seconds a kilometer.

He doesn't look at it as pain..... Just more feedback....

Central governor is hard wired it's not psychological... subconscious theory... Where is it?

Caffeine...
Time trial paced perfect...
Pleasantly fatigued....
Cadence 100 ish...

Efficiently....

Friday 16th may
75 minute turbo lactate threshold.

Saturday 17th may

Sunday 18th may
50 mile time trial. Ran 4.2 miles in 35 minutes.

Monday 19th may
Ran 7.2 miles in 56mins 41seconds.

Tuesday 20th may
Swim 900m warm up. 1500m in 28m 18seconds with paddles. All between 50 and 55 seconds apart from last 50 which was 48seconds. Started at 1m 45 second pace and held it all the way!!

Turbo (110minutes) did 85 minutes. Fitted in before Oscars swimming lesson. Warm up 15. 2 x 230-245watts with 5min recovery in between and 1 x 10m. Warm down 12 minutes.

Wednesday 21st may
Run reps 6 x 1 mile reps

6m 14m, 6m 17, 6m 19, 6m 40, 6m 37, 6m 30.

Thursday 22nd may

4.2km in pool. 900m warm up. 14x200s in 53 minutes. 500m warm down kicks. 1m 54s pace. Breakthrough swim time !!
Quickest length 49secs, only 5 lengths over a minute.

Friday 23rd may
Turbo... Turbo 90 cut it 7 minutes short as big time trial on Sunday

Saturday 24th may
Rest day

Sunday 25th may
100mile tt. 4 hrs 45 minutes. Not bad. Through 25miles in 1 hr 6, 50mikes in 2 hrs 20.. Ran 2.05
Miles afterwards was meant to run five. Felt hot.. When i got home realise i had sunburn !!

Monday 26th may
40m-turbo spin

Tuesday 27th may swim reps.
1800 metre reps in 36 minutes (12x50s, 6x100s, 12x50s).

90minutes turbo! Hard 3x20mins at 230-245 watts

Wednesday 28th may

Run reps. 2 miles warm up...
3 x 1 mile reps. 5m 58, 5m 58, 6m 14
1 1/2 mile warm down

Thursday 29th may
Swim pyramid. 500m warm up breathe drills. 200,400,600,400,200 with paddles. Started at 1m 43m pace ended at 1m 54 pace. 1800 metres in 35 minutes. 500warm down kick chicken wing.

First massage in 3 weeks needed it.

Friday 30th may
Swim lesson Harry Wiltshire in Brockwell lido. First time used wetsuit since September. Fixed right hand. Now stretch when under water and harpoon it pull back, increase cadence, practised siting, swimming round a buoy, drafting from hip and ankles, swimming over somebody on ones back. Doing 1m 35 second

reps. 46secons 50 fastest ever. Slowest was 1m 49 hundreds. Massive improvement - pulling more water back. Stopped pausing right hand. Also told me to relax my feet. Just let go and it will stop me putting breaks on.

30minute turbo in 1 evening.

Not Tight top will lose me 5 minutes in 100mile tt

Saturday 31st of May
12.60 miles in 1 hr 47 mins

Sunday 1st June - rest day

Monday 2nd June - missed turbo. At legoland hotel for 2 days and back at 9pm. that's why I'm not Dave Scott or Mark Allen :)

Tuesday 3rd of June
Swim 900m warm up. 16 x 100s at 32m 5 secs. Started at 1m 53 pace finishes at 1m 59s pace. 45 min eat and then on turbo for 105 mins... 15m warm up 160-200watts. 4 x 15m at 230-245 watts with 5m recovery at 190watts. 15m warm down at 140-179watts. 33.9 miles av sp 18.9 0 gradient.

Wed 4th of June

Run reps. 2 mile warm up. 5x1 mile reps. 1 m recovery. 6m 9, 6m 10, 6m 10, 6m 17, 6m 15.
Felt a bit of a twinge in the evening on groin and hamstring. Got advice from nick.! Let to waking up at 4.00am with pain (pain never came back but slept bad until Sunday night)

Friday 6th June

85-minute turbo. 27.8 miles. 19.6 average speed.
Thu 5th June
500 warm up breathe. 5 x 400s with 45-second rest
and paddles. First ever equal pace paddle set. 7m 32,
7m 29, 7m 26, 7 m 26, 7m 30. 500
Warm down mixed stroke and 1-6-1-kick alternate.

Saturday 6th June

Up early. Double strength coffee at 4.15 am. Couldn't
sleep. Had big work meeting on Wednesday and have
had bad sleep since... Been super productive halftime
and over worrying the next. Exhausted... Started run
b4 breakfast at 5.25 ran

Ran 13.68 miles in 2hrs 5m. Heart rate monitor
stopped working again after 33 minutes when had to
stop for emergency loo next to toilets in a bush as the
toilets in the park were locked...

Saturday 7th-saturday 14th

Wimblewall

Briefing 11-12
Transition
Car park exit only 1-1.30
Car park entry only 1.30-2.00
Another drinks bottle ?!?!?!

Bags:

White bag - bring tomorrow - goggles, wetsuit, cap, (in
registration tent)..... Bum cream....
Bike bag - socks, helmet, bike shoes, belt and number
Red bag run bag - running shoes, cap, shades
Once racked up.... Photograph transition routes....

Where blue bike is..... Off bike... Where is red bag...
Where is run exit...

2 laps of bike, 3 laps of run

Start of bike is uphill...
Timing chip left ankle
Transition manager have time chips...
1st wave 7.00am
6.30am swim transition together...
1 lap clockwise swim - right hand turns...
Mechanics at miles 8 and 33...
Miles 15 and 40.... Careful... Steep decent... 2 yellow
signboards say caution.... Turning left.....

No gels on bike...
Sport bottles on bike cages...
No litter disqualify litter is 50 metres before and after
aid stations.... Throw rubbish on the left only at aid
stations... Loo is at the aid stations !!!

Red bull at run course is half water half red bull... No
littering cups... Use aid stations.... 1.5 miles at each aid
station.... Walk through... Discard only at aid stations....

3 lap run... 4.66 miles each... Race number to front....

Transition bike and bags 9-3.30

Transition race day 5.00am no access to bags but can
go in and put drinks in....

110 psi front 120 back psi....
Ninebar 80grams...

Nick swim 1hr 20, bike 5hr 20, run 3hr 50m.....

Transition 10m - 10hr 40m... (Top 650).

Nick's predicted ironman times....

Wimblewall 70.3
Swim 40m, bike 3hrs 20m run 1hr 50, transitions 8m, 5hrs 58m....
Aim for top 200...

(Electrolyte 800m, pick up electrolyte.... Energy bar, 1 gel)
Gels/water/isotonic....)

My predicted ironman time Frankfurt
Swim 1hr 10m, bike 5hrs 15m, run 3hrs 40m, transitions 6m 10hrs 11minutes.

(Nutrition - 2 bar - 3 energy gels?)

Nick swim 1hr 20, bike 5hr 20, run 3hr 50m.....
Transition 10m - 10hr 40m...

Sunday 15th June

Wimblewall went great - write a few pages here.

Monday 16th of June

Drove back from Wimblewall
Left at 6.30 am back by 11.00am. Gave kids iron kids tips....
Did turbo... Felt good...
Slept like a baby... 12hours... Really deep.... Needed it... Deepest sleep ever and first big sleep for 2 weeks.

Tuesday 17th of June
Did swim reps 12 x 100s started at 1m 53 pace 1m 59

by end. Felt good but fatigued from Sunday. Did 60min turbo was just about to go to sleep so had a second coffee.

Slept like a log again. 10 hours really deep. (Jason's prediction of predicted time on a flat 70.3... Swim 35.... Bike 2 18 Run 1 45.. Transitions 6. 4hrs 44m).

Wednesday 18th of June
Never felt so strong. Reading Mark Allen and Brant Secundas book fit soul fit body 9 keys to a happier healthier you. Slept 10 hours deep last night.
Run reps with nick and Jim today...
Meant to 4 x 1 km reps at 3.30-3.40
But took it easy after half ironman on Sunday. Between 3.40-3.55 reps. could 1 1/2 mile warm up and 2 mile warm down.

Thursday 19th June
Did swim only 2km total
Wu and wd...
Did swim with paddles. 3 x 400s 7m 7, 7 m 34, 7m 20
Finished session by 10.30 wow.

Friday 20th of June
65 minutes turbo held power ok

Saturday 21st June
Looking at houses and took kids to forest

Sunday 22nd of June
90 minute run b4 breakfast 9.8 miles.
Glass of water and creatine and coffee. Felt fine. All in one peace.

Monday 23rd of June
40mins spin 90-110 rpm up to 230

Watts.

Tuesday
Did best swim reps ever. 900m warm up. 16 x 15s in 13m 40seconds. 200m warm down 161 and 131 kick.

Wed
Run reps... 1 1/2 mile warm up. 3 x 1km reps at 3m 35, 3m 37, 3m 36, warm down 1 1/2 mile

Thu
Swim 4 km time trial no aids, no wetsuit in c palace pool. 1hr 26minutes. :)

Friday 27th of June
Last road ride in UK before race. 90 minutes up Biggin hill and back. Only 20 miles. Took it easy never seen so
Many traffic jams, red lights and massive trucks. Wore new shades for new time. Awesome. So clear.

Saturday 28th of June
Nirvana Europe took my bike and kit to Frankfurt at 6.00am and wished me luck.

Sunday 29th of June
Last longish/tempo run. 50mins 6.88 miles round c palace park. 10k in 45 minutes. Was not in the shape running week before race like that last year. Went on feel meant to be between 165-175 heart rate.

Monday 30th June
Run 2.35 mile in 16m 52s. Just over 7m miles. Meant to be 165 steady pace. Whoops.

Tuesday 1st July
Swim 60. 1800m 400 one arm, 500 breathes in 10m 1

sec, 6 x 100s in 12m 1s, 300 warm down - 131/161 kicks with float. Bike 40. Spin.

Wednesday 2nd of July
Flight to Frankfurt... Rest day.... Had to get new passport.... Arrived in Frankfurt 8.20pm. Thank god for nirvana Europe. 20-30 minute walk after got into hotel.

Text from nick

Have a good trip. ...stay focused.
Remember that we know that the training formula works. .....It did for me. ......and it will for you.
It will get tough on second two run laps. .....you already know that. So expect it. When it comes just keep moving, think about consuming just a little gel.....lots of water and pick up and eat some of the salty biscuits or pretzels that they have at the aid stations.....AND KEEP MOVING. ..ALWAYS JOGGING. ...this is the key! Good Race! SOLID RACE!

Thursday 3rd of July
8hrs sleep. Run before breakfast... 22minutes easy pace to check out course and get metabolism right before breakfast.

Breakfast
Bike 52 minutes 15 miles. Never seen so many red lights and so much traffic. 15mins i went 1.29 miles so went on the cycle path after that which was better. Went to media briefing and spoke to some of the pros. Frederick van Lierde,

Spoke to nick on phone talking through race. Texted harry Wiltshire about swim he told he to enjoy and chill out not go too hard and pace it.

Friday 5th of July

Up at 6.00am. 18min easy run in new trainers b4 breakfast. 2.1 Started walking round hotel in them yesterday. Started slow and speeded up a bit... Bit of video diary.... Got autograph of Sebastian Kienle and Jan Frodeno 2008 Olympic champion for Chipmunka foundation . Org and got Frederick Van Lierde to sign my cap as well for the race!! In bed at 7.00. Must have got up 100 times in the night to go to the loo.

Saturday.
Day before race.. Put bike in transition. Left bags on coach... Just got them back in time.. Back in hotel... Ate... In bed at 7.00. Up at 4.30... Hardly slept... Just lay there and kept going to loo.

Sunday...
Race day 12.31. New pb... God it was hot...

Monday...
Awards do. Spoke to Jodie swallow for an hour about 141... Triathlon...

Tuesday
Back home... Nick picked me up... When is next im?

Recovery week....

For best recovery, after a few days off, do 30-40 mins of swim, bike or walk at low HR (less than 135) every other day. On days between do activities that get you up and about and moving that you don't normally do. E.g. Gardening, Wash the car.
Eat plenty of protein, less carbs. Keep hydrated.
Take resting HR every morning to monitor recovery.

I swam 1200m on the Wednesday 40min turbo on the Friday and ran 4 miles on the Sunday... Back in the game... Saw duke in the Saturday... When is next im ? Nick and i going for 1 more year together to hit target time.